W0246691

PUFFIN BOOKS
THE CONSTITUTION OF INDIA FOR CHILDREN

Subhadra Sen Gupta has written over forty books for children because she thinks they are the best readers in the world. She writes about history; loves cooking up mystery, ghost and adventure stories; and dreams up comic books. She was awarded the Bal Sahitya Puraskar by the Sahitya Akademi in 2014.

Tapas Guha is an illustrator who has worked with all the leading publishers. He loves drawing comics and illustrating children's books. His vivid images have delighted children for many years. A master at recreating the past, Tapas has worked on many books about history with Subhadra.

ALSO IN PUFFIN BY SUBHADRA SEN GUPTA

A Flag, a Song and a Pinch of Salt: Freedom Fighters of India
Saffron, White and Green: The Amazing Story of India's Independence
Puffin Lives: Ashoka, the Great and Compassionate King
Puffin Lives: Mahatma Gandhi, the Father of the Nation
The Secret Diary of the World's Worst Cook
Let's Go Time Travelling: Life in India through the Ages
Girls of India: A Mauryan Adventure
The Secret Diary of the World's Worst Friend
A Bagful of History

THE
CONSTITUTION
OF INDIA
FOR CHILDREN

SUBHADRA SEN GUPTA
Illustrations by Tapas Guha

PUFFIN BOOKS

An imprint of Penguin Random House

PUFFIN BOOKS

USA | Canada | UK | Ireland | Australia
New Zealand | India | South Africa | China

Puffin Books is part of the Penguin Random House group of companies
whose addresses can be found at global.penguinrandomhouse.com

Published by Penguin Random House India Pvt. Ltd
4th Floor, Capital Tower 1, MG Road,
Gurugram 122 002, Haryana, India

First published in Puffin Books by Penguin Random House India 2020

Text copyright © Subhadra Sen Gupta 2020
Illustration copyright © Tapas Guha 2020

ISBN 9780143448310

Typeset in Blooms Hand and Archer by Manipal Technologies Limited, Manipal
Book design and layout by Parag Chitale
Printed in India at Acme Print O Pac. Pvt. Ltd. Noida

www.penguin.co.in

CONTENTS

FOR THE PEOPLE OF INDIA

'Swaraj must spring from the wishes of the people of India as expressed through their freely chosen representatives.'

MAHATMA GANDHI

The Constitution of India—it is a phrase you hear often—spoken by solemn experts on television; printed in bold letters on the front page of newspapers and frequently mentioned in history text books. It sounds complicated and hard to understand, doesn't it? How many of us are really very sure what a constitution is? Why do we have one for our country? And most importantly, do we really need to know all about it?

To put it simply, the Constitution of India is a document that lays down the supreme laws of our country.

- It tells us how this country is to be run—in the case of India, it is as a democracy and a republic.
- It states what our rights as citizens are, and also our duties.
- It creates the structure of our government.
- It gives us the right to vote.
- It establishes the framework of our democracy, which is a parliamentary form of government.
- It gives us an independent judiciary.
- It gives us an elected legislature after a free and fair election organized by an independent Election Commission.
- The government is run by an elected legislature and an executive that carries out the will of the people.
- The Constitution speaks for us—the citizens of India.

So it is very important for every Indian to know about it and that includes children.

When described like this, the Constitution sounds like a very complex document, written in a difficult language that only lawyers can understand. In fact, it is thoughtful and liberal, and respects the opinion of the people. Also it is realistic and a surprisingly compassionate piece of writing that is always thinking of the welfare of the Indian citizens—us. It is a document that explains how to protect our rights, make our lives easier and keep us safe and united. The most important thing for the men and women of the Constituent Assembly was to make sure that the Indian citizen had freedom and the right to live in peace and progress in life. An equally important task was to keep India united.

A BIG FAT DOCUMENT

THE CONSTITUTION OF INDIA IS THE LONGEST WRITTEN CONSTITUTION IN THE WORLD. AT PRESENT, IT HAS 448 ARTICLES IN 22 PARTS AND 12 SCHEDULES. OVER THE YEARS, THERE HAVE BEEN 124 AMENDMENTS. THE ORIGINAL DOCUMENT HAD 1,17,369 WORDS, NOW IT HAS 1,46,385 WORDS IN THE ENGLISH VERSION.

IN COMPARISON, THE CONSTITUTION OF MONACO WHICH IS THE SHORTEST WRITTEN CONSTITUTION IN THE WORLD HAS 12 CHAPTERS, 97 ARTICLES AND JUST 3,814 WORDS. AND THE CONSTITUTION OF GREAT BRITAIN IS NOT EVEN WRITTEN DOWN!

All these terms that we find in the Constitution—Parts, Articles, Schedules, Appendices, Amendments . . . what do they mean?

As the Constitution covers many topics these are ways to organize the text and make it easier to understand. As a matter of fact, the Constitution is so complex we have lawyers who are constitutional experts and handle cases on its various aspects.

The Parts are like chapters in a book. For example Part III is about Fundamental Rights and then each part is divided into Articles. The Schedules are additional information, usually of lists, like the lists of States and Union Territories or of Official Languages. Appendices are texts that have been added later. Amendments are changes that have been carried out by the Parliament after 1950.

As you all know, India became independent on 15 August 1947 but at the time, it was not a republic with a constitution. It became a republic on 26 January 1950 when we inaugurated our Constitution. The greatest celebration of the Constitution is our elections, the day when the most important person in the country is the voter—man, woman, rich, poor . . . The first general elections of free India were held between October 1951 and March 1952.

Think of that exciting time when India votes, the colourful images of a democracy at work—men and women standing patiently in long queues; in cities and villages, coming out to celebrate their right to elect their representatives to the Parliament. They are equal, they are free and they have a say in their future. It is our Constitution that has given us equality and the right to vote. This amazing document unites the country while respecting its diversity of region, language and religion. At times, our elections can become quite chaotic, people can get very angry and things can get rather violent. It is not perfect but, to the surprise of the whole world, it has worked pretty well so far.

Our Constitution also promises us justice. When an Indian citizen knocks at the door of the Supreme Court demanding to be heard against any danger to his human rights, especially our Fundamental Rights, it is an appeal to the Constitution.

It also promises us equality and freedom. We have the right to live as free citizens. When we go to a new place to start a new job; join a college in another state; buy land to build our home; marry someone belonging to a different community; pray at a temple, mosque or church or celebrate our festivals in joyous abandon, it is under the protection of our Constitution.

This amazing document, along with its wonderful Preamble, is woven into our lives and very often, we are not even aware of that.

Seventeen years before we gained independence, during our freedom struggle, on 31 December 1929 Jawaharlal Nehru stood on the banks of the River Ravi at Lahore and declared that freedom or swaraj was our only goal. It was decided that from then on, every 26 January would be remembered as Swaraj Day and the first was celebrated all across India in 1930. Twenty years later, in remembrance of that day, we adopted the Constitution of an independent country on 26 January 1950 and

India became a republic and the largest democracy in the world. As the historian Granville Austin writes of the constitution that we created, we ensured, 'Representative government with adult suffrage, a bill of rights providing for equality under the law and personal liberty; and an independent judiciary were to become the spiritual and institutional bases for a new country.'

The journey has not been easy. We have struggled with poverty and illiteracy, wars and famines. There are also the challenges of what can still divide us—the horrors of the caste system that still exists after it was made illegal by the Constitution; the complexities of many languages; of religion being used by political parties to create divisions and huge disparities in the economic conditions of the people where we have some of the richest people in the world as well as some of the poorest.

What is amazing is how the country has remained united and how we have persevered in chasing the dream that began in 1947. We put those dreams into our Constitution and have held on to its promise for all these years. Every year, on a chilly January morning, people have gathered on New Delhi's Rajpath to celebrate Republic Day in a colourful jamboree of fluttering flags, marching soldiers and dancing children.

So every Republic Day, we are in fact, celebrating what lies at the heart of our democracy—the magnificent Constitution of India.

Pandit Jawaharlal Nehru was part of the Constituent Assembly that worked for three years to write the

Constitution of India and he influenced its wide ranging, democratic, liberal, tolerant and compassionate character. Scholar, writer, dreamer and beloved of the people, he was much more than a political leader; he was our conscience and the hope of a new nation. He was well aware that for the first time in over two centuries, we Indians were responsible for our own governance.

At midnight, before the dawn of our Independence Day on 15 August 1947, Nehru spoke these poetic, passionate and unforgettable words. Finally the Indians were free after centuries of colonization and the country had exploded in wild celebration. Here is an extract from his famous speech that we call 'Tryst with Destiny'. Read it carefully, and discover what we mean by the Indian spirit of courage, tolerance and hope, qualities that have kept India united.

Long years ago we made a tryst with destiny, and now the time comes when we shall redeem our pledge, not wholly or in full measure, but very substantially. At the stroke of the midnight hour, when the world sleeps, India will awake to life and freedom.

A moment comes, which comes but rarely in history, when we step out from the old to the new, when an age ends, and when the soul of a nation, long suppressed, finds utterance. It is fitting that at this solemn moment we take the pledge of dedication to the service of India and her people and to the still larger cause of humanity...

Freedom and power bring responsibility. That responsibility rests upon this Assembly, a sovereign body representing the sovereign people of India ... That future is not one of ease or resting but of incessant striving so that we might fulfil the pledges we have so often taken and the one we shall take today. The service of India means the service of the millions who suffer. It means the ending of poverty and ignorance and disease and inequality of opportunity. The ambition of the greatest man of our generation has been to wipe every tear from every eye. That may be beyond us but as long as there are tears and suffering, so long our work will not be over ...

To the people of India, whose representatives we are, we make the appeal to join us with faith and confidence in this great adventure. This is no time for petty and destructive criticism, no time for ill will or blaming others. We have to build the noble mansion of free India where all her children may dwell.

Writing a complicated document like a constitution that was so important for the future of the country was hard enough but the members of the Constituent Assembly faced many other challenges. The drafting of the Constitution took three years from 1946 to 1949 with long sessions of debates in the Assembly. Meanwhile, during the same period, what was happening outside the Assembly was a huge, violent social upheaval—the Partition of India.

During the 1940s, as India came closer to gaining independence, the demand by the Muslim League for a separate nation for Muslims grew louder and communal riots spread across north India. Then, after independence and the terrible tragedy of a country being divided on the basis of religion, the Partition led to a huge exodus of people on both sides. And in spite of the efforts of Mahatma Gandhi and Nehru, thousands died.

So as the members of the Constituent Assembly argued and discussed different articles of the Constitution in the Parliament, on the other side of their door, refugees were pouring into Delhi, carrying tales of unbelievable horror. The government was struggling to control riots while also housing and feeding the refugees. The fact that the Constitution was still drafted and passed shows the determination of our leaders.

So this book is not just a dry as dust explanation of the various articles and schedules of the Constitution, it is also about the people who laboured with extraordinary courage and dedication to produce it. It is not just about the men who are, in our minds, connected to the Constitution like B.R. Ambedkar, Jawaharlal Nehru and Maulana Azad. It is also about the quiet voices like Durgabai Deshmukh, who fought for the rights of women and Jaipal Singh, who spoke for the tribal people. Also the backroom boys like B.N. Rau, an expert on constitutions and Drafting Officer S.N. Mukherjee, who did the actual work of research and drafting. The creators of the Constitution were great patriots.

The Constitution was not the work of a few famous leaders; it was a team effort and every member of the Assembly was crucial to its conception. It is the story of a remarkable group of men and women who often held very different views, who would argue and disagree,

xvii

but always thought of the country and saw fit to work together, choosing consensus over politics. For them, the Constitution was for the benefit of the whole country, not that of any specific community, religion or caste. What was important was the citizen of India and the nation always came first. In this book, we will read about the achievements of many forgotten heroes of the Constituent Assembly.

The Constitution that they produced was both an optimistic and a realistic one and also a proudly Indian document. No one was harking back to the past as they all agreed that it was to be a modernizing force to take our backward country into a better future. It spoke about genuine values of humanity; of equality and secularism; of human rights and democracy. They wanted the Constitution to unite people, not divide them and that is why it has survived for so many years.

Another important factor was that they had known the trauma of a country being divided over religion and they all understood that it was India's unity that was crucial. India was the first colonized nation that had fought and gained freedom and a very doubtful world, especially the western countries, was watching, waiting for us to fail. The western countries thought that we could not bring democracy, social and economic progress to such a poor and socially fractured country simply by writing a constitution. The assembly members knew this and we were fortunate to get an absolute pantheon of truly great leaders who made sure we got a constitution that would take India forward.

Just a list of the members of the constituent assembly reads like an honour roll of achievement and greatness.

They were men and women of every political belief, belonging to various religions, of different castes and class but they all understood one crucial fact—that we had to keep the country together and that to remain united, every Indian had to be treated with equal respect. You are a nationalist when you think of all the citizens of India and you are a patriot when our rainbow nation comes before all else. And this feeling of deep love for India and respect for all its citizens permeates our Constitution.

VOICES

'THE KEY QUESTION REMAINS: CAN INDIA REMAIN IN ONE PIECE—OR WILL IT FRAGMENT? . . . WHEN ONE LOOKS AT THIS VAST COUNTRY . . . IT SEEMS INCREDIBLE THAT ONE NATION COULD EMERGE . . . AND YET THERE IS A RESILIENCE ABOUT INDIA WHICH SEEMS AN ASSURANCE OF SURVIVAL. THERE IS SOMETHING WHICH CAN ONLY BE DESCRIBED AS AN INDIAN SPIRIT. I BELIEVE IT NO EXAGGERATION TO SAY THAT THE FATE OF ASIA HANGS ON ITS SURVIVAL.'—DON TAYLOR, BRITISH JOURNALIST, WRITING IN 1969.

The Constitution of India is not perfect. After all, the members of the Assembly could not anticipate every challenge of the future. Since the Constitution was adopted, there have been times when our democracy has been threatened and seemed very fragile but the people have stood up against such threats and held on to their rights. Even the poorest farmer or a barely literate tribal woman understands democracy very well and we have all made it work. When we read our Constitution, we can listen to the wise words of our great leaders and we can make sure that this great adventure for democracy flourishes.

CHAPTER ONE

WHAT IS A CONSTITUTION?

'The wheels of fate will someday compel the English to give up their Indian Empire. But what kind of India will they leave behind, what stark misery?'

RABINDRANATH TAGORE

Rabindranath Tagore, the poet laureate of our freedom movement did not live to see India become free but his words echo what many felt about the ruins that the British would leave behind when India became independent. Could such a nation even dream of democracy and a constitution?

What would our great leaders think of the India of today? From the inspiring Mahatma Gandhi and Rabindranath Tagore to the architects of our Constitution—Jawaharlal Nehru, B.R. Ambedkar, Maulana Azad, Sardar Patel, Sarojini Naidu, et al.—men and women have been described by historian Bipan Chandra as, 'dedicated, imaginative and idealistic'. Some things might have made them happy, and perhaps some angry but as realists, little of the story of Independent India would have surprised them. As Nehru wrote, 'With the end of slavery and the dawn of freedom, all the weaknesses of society are bound to come to the surface', and our politics—that is now often corrupt, violent, at times borders on the criminal—has proved him right. To keep India democratic, equal, tolerant and civilized, our only hope is our Constitution.

In 1950, pessimists were sure that India would fail. Some said that India was so poor it could not even feed its people and here were its leaders, dreaming of a constitution. The western countries were even more sceptical; *how could a poor Asian country of illiterate brown people even understand what it means to be a democracy or what a constitution is*, they wondered. An American scholar Selig S. Harrison wrote gloomily in the 1960s, 'the odds are almost wholly against the survival of freedom . . . the issue is, in fact, whether any Indian state can survive at all.' The journalist Neville Maxwell wrote a pessimistic article in the Times, titled, 'India's Disintegrating Democracy', in which he claimed that 'The great experiment of developing India within a democratic framework has failed' and then went on to predict that the election of 1967 will be India's last election! As we celebrate our Constitution, we have certainly proved the naysayers wrong, haven't we?

It wasn't as if our leaders sat down one day and said, 'Let's write a constitution', they had been preparing for years and knew what they were doing. What the critics forgot was that India is a very old civilization and we do have a tradition of democracy and republics. In ancient India, during the time of the Buddha, we had kingdoms called Mahajanapadas and among them were republics of the Lichhavi and Malla tribes, which were ruled by groups of people instead of a king. Our panchayat system, where we have five people elected by a village to run the administration, has been there for centuries and Gandhiji was greatly in favour of a constitution based around village panchayats. Ambedkar spoke of the Buddhist monasteries, which had governing assemblies called the Sangha, and therefore were democratic systems. We may have had maharajas and nawabs but we also always had some basic forms of democracy.

Most importantly, the Congress Party had always been a democratic organization and had trained its members in the practises of democracy. When Mahatma Gandhi became its leader, he and his team opened the doors of the party to everyone. All you had to do was pay a small fee of four annas and you were a Congress Party member. At party meetings, members could vote for the various committees and resolutions and have a say in the working of the party. Everyone had a right to speak and had a vote and no one checked if you were rich or poor, what your educational background was or what your religion was. Soon the party flag was flying over village huts as people realized that they could vote and voice their opinion. The thinking on what independent India was to be had been going on for decades and some of the finest political and legal minds like G.K Gokhale and Dadabhai Naoroji had been writing about it.

Very gradually and reluctantly, some democratic rights had also been given to Indians by the British government through acts like the Minto-Morley Act of 1909 and the Government of India Act of 1935 after which there were elections. Of course, most people were not allowed to vote and the elected members of the assemblies had little power. Still, the political parties had fought elections, formed governments and learnt valuable lessons about how to run them. As our leaders wisely understood, you did not need a university degree to understand democracy. You just had to be free to vote.

The tragedy was that by the time the new constitution was unveiled, India had lost its voice of morality, conscience and inspiration. Mahatma Gandhi was no more because on 30 January 1948, he had been assassinated by a man who believed in the right wing ideology of communal organizations that wanted a Hindu nation where people of other religions would be treated as second class citizens. This was something that Bapu had fought against all his life. But his spirit of tolerance, dedication to social justice and non-violence permeates the constitution.

The inspiring words of the Preamble of the Constitution are like Gandhiji's gentle reminder of what we want our country and our society to be. Of course, everything he said, and he had made many suggestions, was not incorporated into the Constitution because this was a democratic assembly and everything was done by vote and consensus. Gandhiji would not have had any problem with that.

It All Begins with a Constitution

There are all these words that can confuse us sometimes because they can mean so many things—constitution, republic, democracy, act of Parliament, etc. And how do they all work? As we study our Constitution, we will begin to understand what they stand for. You may also ask, is it really that important to have a constitution?

You will agree that every society needs laws. Without laws, there would be chaos. The powerful, the rich and the criminal would be free to use their power to control our lives. When a rich man tries to grab the land of a farmer, a crooked finance company embezzles people's money or when an industrialist refuses to pay factory workers a living wage, laws come to the aid of people. We can go to the police, appeal to the courts and rely on the laws to protect us.

At the same time, we need a government. We not only need a prime minister and ministers who run different departments like home affairs, health and education in the Central government, but also state governments and government officers in towns and villages. From the magistrate to the post master to the nurse at the health clinic, they are all part of the government. We also need police officers and law courts with judges to make the laws work. We need a free press that will give us the correct news and independent writers who will write about the realities of the country. An executive appointed by an elected Parliament, an independent judiciary, an election commission ensuring free and fair elections and a free press are the pillars that hold up a democracy. We understand that very well and that is why people protest so fiercely when any of these pillars are in danger.

LISTEN TO HAMMURABI

PEOPLE REALIZED PRETTY EARLY THAT SOCIETY NEEDS LAWS. THE FIRST CIVILIZATION ROSE IN MESOPOTAMIA (MODERN IRAQ) AND HERE, IN 1792 BCE, HAMMURABI BECAME THE KING OF BABYLON AND HE WAS SO POWERFUL HE WAS CALLED THE 'KING OF THE FOUR QUARTERS'. HE WAS THE FIRST KING TO CREATE LAWS THAT HIS SUBJECTS HAD TO OBEY AND ALSO STATED THE PUNISHMENT FOR PEOPLE WHO BROKE THE LAWS. THESE 282 LAWS COVERED EVERYTHING FROM DIVORCE AND WAGES TO BE PAID TO LABOURERS TO THE CORRECT FEES FOR DOCTORS. THE LAWS WERE ENGRAVED ON STONE SLABS CALLED 'STELA' AND SOME HAVE SURVIVED TILL TODAY.

So we needed a constitution to lay it down in writing the rules and laws that would govern the country. It tells us how people will elect a Parliament and how the members of Parliament would choose a government. We would have an independent judiciary and an election commission, so that the Parliament, the executive or the army do not grab all the power and turn the government into a dictatorship. As an example of how our Constitution protects our rights, let us consider the time when a state of Emergency was declared in 1975, causing our fundamental rights to be put on hold—people were arrested without warrants, there were no trials and the press was censored so people could not get the correct news. No one was allowed to protest. At the next elections, in 1977, the people answered by voting out the government of Indira Gandhi. Another example of our Constitution in action is the Supreme Court declaring that the gay community had the freedom to live openly, while the government wanted to treat them like criminals. This is how the Constitution protects the rights of the people.

In such a huge and complicated country like India, with so many religions, languages and regions, what unites us is the Constitution. It speaks for everyone. There was a time, before our independence, when people claimed many identities based on their religion or language—for example, they would say they were Tamil Brahmans or Gujarati Jains—but now we can proudly say we are Indians first.

However, the Constitution is as effective as we make it. We have to treat it with respect and protest loudly when someone in power tries to change it for their own benefit. Political parties are often tempted to defy the Constitution because of their hunger for power. During elections, they might challenge the Constitution merely to get votes and win. They may try to gather all the power for themselves and deny the rights of people who have not supported them, like some organizations that claim that anyone who does not belong to the religion of the majority does not have the same rights. Remember that using religion or caste to get votes is unconstitutional and against our laws.

You know that we Indians like to protest and ask questions and that is a good thing. During the freedom movement, people had demanded freedom and democracy, which not only led to them facing the police but even giving up their lives. They had learnt to question and be disobedient and to fight for their rights. We see it even today, when thousands of farmers walk for hundreds of kilometres in a peaceful protest to make the government listen to them. They were saying very politely, that if you do not listen to us, then we will not vote for you. So we have to protect our unity and equality and the rights that the constitution gives us but we can only do so if we are aware of what it says. As citizens of this country, it is of the utmost importance that we understand and fight for this great charter.

WORDS AND IMAGES

THE FIRST TWO SETS, IN ENGLISH AND HINDI, OF THE CONSTITUTION OF INDIA WERE HANDWRITTEN IN EXQUISITE CALLIGRAPHY BY PREM BEHARI AND NARAIN RAIZADA. THERE WERE ALSO BEAUTIFUL ILLUSTRATIONS BY A TEAM OF ARTISTS LED BY THE FAMOUS PAINTER FROM SANTINIKETAN, NANDALAL BOSE.

One Citizen, One Vote

The Constituent Assembly began with one absolute premise—India was going to be a democracy where power would be vested in the hands of the people. There were many suggestions and discussions about the form of government but when it came to universal adult suffrage, that is a vote for every adult, no one ever questioned that. The inspiration for the Constitution can be found in India's hard fought struggle to gain independence. Our freedom movement was the largest mass movement in the world and always, the spirit of democracy was inherent in it.

The members of the Constituent Assembly, many of whom were eminent scholars and lawyers, studied the constitutions of many countries like the Unites States of America, the United Kingdom of Great Britain, France, Ireland and Russia. They had many forms of government to choose from—a monarchy, a presidential form of government, a republic, a one-party dictatorship, etc. We chose the parliamentary form of government. The influences were many but at the end, our Constitution is Indian in spirit as it addresses the unique challenges of our country. Of course, it was going to be hard.

The Constitution is not just a political and legal document talking about how India is to be run and how justice is to be provided to the people. It is also a social and economic document that lays down the fundamental rights of the people, states the duties of the government in the Directive Principles and bans social evils like untouchability and bonded labour. Our leaders were not just freedom fighters, they were also social activists and leaders.

The Preamble states what is called the 'basic structure' of the Constitution and the Supreme Court has made it clear that it cannot be changed. Any attempt to do so can be challenged in the Supreme Court. It speaks clearly and simply about the nation's goals, the rights of its citizens and spells out what lies at the core of the Constitution, what Granville Austin calls, 'the three strands of a seamless web'—unity, social revolution and democracy. In 1947, after the partition of the country the members of the Muslim League left to form their own Constituent Assembly in Pakistan. At this point, the Congress Party had over 80 per cent of the seats in the Assembly. If they had wanted, they could have voted for a one-party dictatorship like the Soviet Republic and China. In these countries, the Communist party rules forever and people have few rights but our enlightened leaders chose not to do so.

Over the years, the Indian Constitution has been a modernizing force that has helped transform India. It is not perfect, but in spite of its flaws and the many challenges it has faced over the years, it has worked remarkably well so far.

Same Beginnings, Different Paths

In 1947, India and Pakistan began their journeys in identical conditions, economically and socially, but in the last seven decades, their history has taken very different paths. The biggest difference between the two countries was that India chose secularism where all religions are given equal respect while Pakistan chose to become an Islamic republic.

Today, India and Pakistan have little in common beyond a shared past as they have created their own political, social and economic stories. One of the reasons has been the constitution that each country adopted. India inaugurated its one and only constitution in 1950 and while there may have been amendments over the years, the core of the document, which is its spirit of democracy based on equality, human rights, voting rights for all and secularism, has not changed.

The members of the Muslim League left the Constituent Assembly in India after the formation of Pakistan and a sixty-nine-member assembly was formed in Pakistan. M.A. Jinnah advocated a two nation theory that contributed towards the partitioning of British India into Pakistan and India on the basis of religion. Strangely enough, he imagined a secular Pakistan and died soon after. Soon, the assembly began to debate the role of Islam in the running of the new country; this was no surprise since they had divided the country on the basis of religion. The Pakistani assembly's slow speed gave an impression that the leaders were not too serious about producing a constitution.

The difference between the Congress Party and the Muslim League was that the Congress was always a democratic party. Everything was discussed and then voted on and every member had the vote. In the Muslim League, the leaders came from the rich landowning class who had feudal ideas about society where the poor or even women had no rights. So these rich men and Jinnah dictated its actions. To give you a simple example of their difference in attitude—during the freedom movement, Jinnah never led a protest march while all the Congress leaders were facing the police lathis and going to prison. The Muslim League demanded a new country without fighting for India's freedom.

It took nine years before Pakistan was declared an 'Islamic Republic' in 1956, which meant that minority communities like Hindus and Christians were not given equal rights, and this was something Jinnah had not wanted. In 1962, General Ayub Khan declared that most Pakistanis were not ready for democracy and in a new constitution, actually reduced the number of people who were allowed to vote! They were only to choose a President and not a parliament so that it was giving power to a dictatorship.

The first general elections were held in Pakistan only in 1970, and by then, Indians had been voting for eighteen years. The Bangladesh War followed in 1971 when Mujibur Rahman of East Pakistan, who had won the elections, was not allowed to become prime minister and Bangladesh rebelled and gained independence. In 1973, a new constitution made religion more important for the nation and in 1977, Muhammad Zia-ul-Haq replaced the existing laws with ancient sharia laws.

The weakness of the constitution of Pakistan has allowed the army to dominate politics and thus, ignore democracy and the rights of the people. As Pakistan declared it was an Islamic nation, it led to terrorist organizations wielding power by using religion. So if you compare the constitutions of India and Pakistan, the biggest difference is that every adult Indian has the right to vote; we elect our government by regular elections and people of all religions are treated as equal before the law. In India, when we speak of secularism, what we mean is that people are free to follow any religion they want, the laws respect all religions equally but religion does not dictate the laws. Pakistan may call itself a republic and a democracy but when free and fair elections are not held regularly and the law treats people differently according to religion and gender, it is not a democracy.

India in 1950

If you could go back in time and see what India was like in 1950, you will get an idea of what we faced as a new nation and also what we have achieved so far. It was quite a scary picture. What is remarkable is how courageous and optimistic the people and our leaders were. The mood was buoyant with hope at midnight on 25 January 1950, when people went out in a happy procession to the Parliament, carrying torches, singing and celebrating. Delhi glowed with streams of lights, sparkling along the streets and the Indian flag adorned every rooftop.

In the morning—at the durbar hall in the building that was once the residence of the British viceroy—C. Rajagopalachari, the outgoing Governor-General, and Rajendra Prasad, the new President, sat on the dais before the image of the Buddha that stands there even today. The Chief Justice administrated the oath of office to the President as the guns boomed outside in a thirty-one-gun salute and the national anthem echoed through the hallways of the building that was now called Rashtrapati Bhawan.

The time for what Nehru called 'incessant striving' had begun.

What was India like on 26 January 1950? During the time of the Mughals, India had been one of the biggest economies in the world but after two centuries of British colonization, we were among the poorest. The British had economically exploited the country in every manner possible. Nearly 82 per cent of the population lived in villages and farmers were taxed the most. Rich people like bureaucrats, industrialists and landowners, many of whom were British, hardly paid any taxes. Nothing was done to improve agriculture, farmers were still using the primitive wooden plough and they had no access to fertilizers. There were no irrigation projects like dams or canals being built by the government. Farmers were at the mercy of landowners and money lenders and the production of food crops was falling. There were famines, the worst being the famine in 1942 in Bengal, during which 30 lakh people died because of neglect by the government, which was more occupied with the Second World War. In 1950, we did not grow enough food crops to feed our people and were dependent on imports and aid from western countries.

BOUNTY OF CROPS

AFTER CENTURIES OF NEGLECTING AGRICULTURE, IN THE LAST FIFTY YEARS OF BRITISH RULE, THE PRODUCTION OF FOOD CROPS WAS GOING DOWN. WITHIN JUST THREE YEARS OF INDEPENDENCE, AGRICULTURE BEGAN TO GROW AT 3 PER CENT PER YEAR.

The colonizers levied high taxes to discourage Indians from starting industries while the country's textile industry, which had once dominated world trade, was systematically ruined so that British mills could buy our raw cotton for cheap and then sell us its dull factory-made textiles. The Congress campaign, in support of khadi, was an answer to this. If you study the photographs of our leaders at the Constituent Assembly, most of them are clad in khadi and the most eye-catching is Sarojini Naidu in her gorgeous handwoven silks and cottons.

Today we have factories making everything from cars and instant noodles to mobile phones and medicines. In 1950, all we produced were bicycles and sewing machines. The British may have built roads but very few people had cars and no one even knew the phrase, 'stuck in a traffic jam'. Hardly anything was made in India as the British wanted Indians to buy their products. We were even importing biscuits and shoes during the British period. You can't imagine the level of illiteracy—there were no primary schools in most villages. In 1951, 84 per cent of the men and 92 per cent women could not read or write but by the 2011 census, India's literacy level stood at 74 per cent and Delhi had the highest at 86 per cent. One of the reasons our political parties were given symbols during the first elections was because voters could not read a ballot paper.

There were few hospitals and no rural health service and the average age of Indians was just thirty-two years. There were epidemics like cholera and small pox as there was no sanitation system and even towns had open drains.

So all the members of the Constituent Assembly had these social and economic issues in mind when drafting the country's most important document. The Constitution is much more than a legal document that tells us of the structure of our government. It is also a remarkable act of social reform that offered the poorest citizen equality and a voice in the Parliament. It gave reservation in education and jobs to the Dalits and an opportunity to progress.

It reassured people of every religion that they were free to follow any faith they chose and just as important—chose not to follow any religion at all, declaring yourself an atheist when they come to your home for the census. Just as you can say that you are a transgender.

For centuries, our colonizers tried to convince us that we were a backward nation without any culture or heritage and that the western countries had colonized us to bring progress and civilization. They were very good at giving Indians an inferiority complex. The freedom movement taught us to be proud again and when we marched out on streets carrying the tricolour, we stopped being afraid. The members of the Constituent Assembly, overflowing with ideas, arguing and discussing, objecting and compromising, reflected this sense of independence. It was a surprisingly optimistic group of people sharing a great spirit of cooperation.

With the adoption of the Constitution, India became the largest democracy in the world and today, its long and complex elections capture the attention of the world. The Preamble captures this spirit of political independence, economic progress and social reform when it states categorically that we are a free and democratic nation that proudly promotes liberty, equality, fraternity and secularism. We have come far in the last several decades and to go on with our progress, we have to hold on to the values enshrined in that amazing document that is the Constitution of India.

Our future depends on it.

CHAPTER TWO

THE PREAMBLE

'It was indeed, a way of life,
which recognizes liberty, equality,
and fraternity as the principles of life
which cannot be divorced from
each other . . .'

B.R. AMBEDKAR ON THE PREAMBLE

22

The first page of the Constitution of India is called the Preamble. A Preamble is an introduction to any piece of writing like a book or document. On that first page, in deeply thought out and beautifully phrased words, it introduces us to the document that would follow and captures the spirit and philosophy of the Constitution.

The Preamble to the Constitution begins with the words, 'We, the People of India . . .', and it is speaking for every Indian. It is the voice of a people who had been enslaved for over two hundred years, who were now standing tall and declaring to the world, 'Listen! This is our Constitution, we are writing it for the people of our country.' Even after all these years, it fills our hearts with pride as we declared with surprising optimism and confidence that this is the voice of an independent nation.

SUBHADRA SEN GUPTA

This is one page every Indian should read as the Preamble establishes the guiding principles of the Constitution. It lays down the basic structure of the Constitution and is the 'heart and soul' of the Constitution. As Derek O'Brien says, 'The Preamble lays down the national goals, and states the aims and ideals of the nation.' It states in clear, unequivocal terms what it plans to achieve. With simplicity and courage, it states what the future of India will be. After decades of dreaming of such a nation, our founders put their aspirations into these beautiful words and today it reads:

THE CONSTITUTION OF INDIA

WE, THE PEOPLE OF INDIA having solemnly resolved to constitute India into a SOVEREIGN, SOCIALIST, SECULAR, DEMOCRATIC REPUBLIC and to secure to all its citizens:
JUSTICE, social, economic and political;
LIBERTY of thought, expression, belief, faith and worship;
EQUALITY of status and of opportunity;
And to promote among them all,
FRATERNITY assuring the dignity of the individual and the unity and integrity of the nation;
IN OUR CONSTITUENT ASSEMBLY this twenty-sixth day of November, 1949, do HEREBY ADOPT, ENACT AND GIVE OURSELVES THIS CONSTITUTION.

The Preamble is the final word on any ambiguities in the Constitution and it is the guiding spirit of our laws. It is also a pledge, promising the citizens of a democratic country—justice, liberty and equality.

THE 42ND AMENDMENT

THE ORIGINAL PREAMBLE DESCRIBED INDIA AS 'SOVEREIGN, DEMOCRATIC REPUBLIC'. THE 42ND AMENDMENT OF 1976 ADDED THE WORDS, 'SOCIALIST', 'SECULAR' AND AT THE END, IN THE LINE ON FRATERNITY, THE WORD, 'INTEGRITY'.

What we should always remember is that this is a constitution that we Indians gave ourselves. It was not handed down to us by any colonial power or any monarch. The Preamble is like a paean to our long struggle to gain freedom. And it says it all clearly, that power is now vested in the Indian people.

Words like *fraternity, sovereign* and *socialism* can buzz around in our heads and at times, we find them rather hard to understand. Most of us have a vague knowledge of even words like justice or liberty. So let's look at all the ideas that have been mentioned in the Preamble, check what they mean in a dictionary and then try to understand how they affect our lives. They may seem complicated but if we connect them to our lives, they are quite easy to understand. And you can be sure of one thing—they are all important for our happiness not just today, but for all future generations of Indians.

We, the People of India

It is the most beautiful phrase in the Preamble, as a people who had been colonized, exploited and had their spirits broken finally raised their heads and said proudly, 'We, the people of India . . .' and the whole world had to listen. It is the inspiration and spirit of the Constitution.

You may be surprised to hear this but when the Constitution says, 'We the people of India', it includes every citizen of the country including children. Yes! Children too! Yes, children below the age of eighteen cannot vote, but that does not mean they do not have the same rights. Take the right to education, which is a fundamental right—each child has a right to go to school. For example, if a village does not have a primary school, then the government can be asked to provide one. Also, anyone of the age of eighteen is allowed to vote and—think about it—at eighteen, you are still a teenager.

Read the words carefully—it says, 'We, the *people* of India' not 'We the Hindus of India' or 'We the men of India'. Everyone has equal rights and it does not matter if you are a man, woman or child; what religion you follow; which region you live in; what language you speak; what your income is; what you eat; what you wear; and what you do. Our Constitution has made that very clear, right on the first page, that the future belongs to you. It is wide open with opportunities, you are free and equal so go ahead and march out to follow your dream.

ANOTHER PREAMBLE

THE PREAMBLE TO THE CONSTITUTION OF THE USA OF 1789 SAYS, 'WE THE PEOPLE OF THE UNITED STATES, IN ORDER TO FORM A MORE PERFECT UNION, ESTABLISH JUSTICE, INSURE DOMESTIC TRANQUILLITY, PROVIDE FOR THE COMMON DEFENCE, PROMOTE THE GENERAL WELFARE, AND SECURE THE BLESSINGS OF LIBERTY TO OURSELVES AND OUR POSTERITY, DO ORDAIN AND ESTABLISH THIS CONSTITUTION FOR THE UNITED STATES OF AMERICA.'

VOICES

'I AM AMAZED AT WHAT OUR CONSTITUTION-MAKERS HAVE ACCOMPLISHED. THE AMERICANS TALKED ABOUT LIFE, LIBERTY AND ALL SORTS OF HAPPINESS WHEN THEY SET UP THEIR CONSTITUTION AND WE TALK ABOUT EQUALITY, LIBERTY. IN SOME SENSE, THAT IDEALISM IS REALLY WHAT ACTS AS A CHECK-AND-BALANCE AGAINST ITS ABUSE. THAT'S THE GREATEST OF WHAT HAS BEEN CREATED.'—NANDAN NILEKANI

Sovereign

At one time, a king was referred to as a sovereign and he was treated as a supreme ruler who possessed absolute powers. A king would claim that all the land belonged to him and all the people were his subjects and therefore, had to obey him. Now, we are a republic and the people are that sovereign power and so, we are not subject to the control of any monarch, other state or external power. This meant that the king-emperor of Great Britain was no longer our ruler and he and the British government could no longer tell us what to do. They could not impose taxes on us or send our young men to fight in wars. Now the monarch of the United Kingdom was just the king of a tiny island in Europe and we could happily ignore him and his government. In all our dealings with other countries, it is our elected government that speaks for us.

Socialist

Socialism is a political and economic theory that says that the means of production and distribution should be owned or regulated by the community. How does that work? It means we have equal rights to all the products and services of our country. We have a right to food and clothing, homes, education, health care and the use of services like hospitals, schools, roads and railways. No one can say that you cannot live in this area, do this job, use this hospital or buy these products.

Secular

This is a word that often leads to controversy and misunderstanding because it is very hard to explain. The dictionary says secular means, 'not being religious, sacred or spiritual'. However, in the Indian Constitution, it has a different meaning. Think of all the religions practiced by Indians—Hinduism, Islam, Christianity, Jainism, Buddhism, Sikhism, Zoroastrianism, Bahai and Judaism. It is very important for peace and unity that everyone should be free to follow their own religion.

So, unlike Pakistan, India has no state religion. Our schools do not have classes on religion. We cannot pass any law in favour of any one religion. The government treats all religions equally and it does not have the right to show any preference to any one religion. Alexander Owics explains secularism, as practiced in India, as, 'Secularism is a part of the basic structure of the Indian Constitution and it means equal freedom and respect for all religions.'

Secularism is very important for India because we are a religious people and it is always tempting for political parties to support only people of one faith to get their votes. According to our Constitution, religion is a personal matter and the government has to stay out of it. As history has shown across the world, when we let religion enter our political lives, what follows is a lack of unity and violence as people are divided according to their faith because religious and political leaders encourage hate for their own profit. All religions teach of love and kindness but ambitious people will use religion to divide and spread hate. Be very suspicious of anyone claiming to speak for any religion; your faith should be your personal choice and not dictated by anyone else.

S. RADHAKRISHNAN ON SECULARISM

SARVEPALLI RADHAKRISHNAN, WHO BECAME THE SECOND PRESIDENT OF INDIA, WAS A RENOWNED SCHOLAR OF INDIAN PHILOSOPHY AND AUTHORED MANY BOOKS ON THE VEDAS AND UPANISHADS. HERE, HE EXPLAINS HOW SECULARISM IS A PART OF ANCIENT INDIAN THOUGHT.

HE SAYS, 'WE HOLD THAT NOT ONE RELIGION SHOULD BE GIVEN PREFERENTIAL STATUS, OR UNIQUE DISTINCTION . . . NO GROUP OF CITIZENS SHALL ARROGATE TO ITSELF RIGHTS AND PRIVILEGES THAT IT DENIES TO OTHERS. NO PERSON SHOULD SUFFER ANY FORM OF DISABILITY OR DISCRIMINATION BECAUSE OF HIS RELIGION BUT ALL ALIKE SHOULD BE FREE TO SHARE TO THE FULLEST DEGREE IN THE COMMON LIFE . . . SECULARISM AS HERE DEFINED IS IN ACCORDANCE WITH THE ANCIENT RELIGIOUS TRADITION OF INDIA.'

Democratic

A democracy is a form of government where the people have power—typically through elected representatives. We vote, our chosen representatives become the members of Parliament and the political party that has won the maximum number of seats then elects a prime minister and the prime minister appoints his cabinet of ministers—that is a democracy. After five years, we go back to the ballot to choose our government again and if we are unhappy with the party in power, we have the right to vote against it.

As we have all learnt the phrase in school, a democracy is, 'of the people, for the people and by the people'.

GETTYSBURG ADDRESS

THE PHRASE 'OF THE PEOPLE, BY THE PEOPLE, FOR THE PEOPLE' WAS FIRST USED BY US PRESIDENT ABRAHAM LINCOLN ON 19 NOVEMBER 1863, DURING HIS FAMOUS SPEECH AT GETTYSBURG.

Republic

A republic is a state in which supreme power is held by the people and people elect their representatives, the members of Parliament (MPs) and state legislative assemblies (MLAs). In fact, all appointment to public office like a municipality or village panchayat has to be done through elections.

It can be a bit confusing because even in a republic, the kind of government can be a bit different in different countries. For example, in the United States of America, the government is led by a President but in Great Britain and India, it is led by the Prime Minister. Great Britain still has a queen, but she has no powers and does not choose the prime minister—the elected Parliament does that. It is the Parliament that makes the laws. Our Parliament has two houses—the Lok Sabha and the Rajya Sabha.

Justice

The first promise the Constitution makes is to, 'secure for all its citizens JUSTICE, social, economic and political'. Justice means behaving justly, that is, in a morally correct and fair manner. Justice is mentioned first in the Preamble because it is a right that is crucial for our happiness and prosperity. It means that all citizens are treated as equal before the law.

Our right to justice has been stated loud and clear because, as history has shown many times, the rich and powerful people will always try to get special treatment. They will always try to exploit the poor and powerless and getting justice is not easy. For example, the Unites States constitution may have talked of justice but as long as they had slavery, African Americans had no rights and there was no real justice in their country. In India, as long as the Dalits or women are denied their rights as equal citizens, we do not have justice either. So remember, when we stand up and ask for justice against any form of oppression, our Constitution stands beside us.

LIBERTY, EQUALITY, FRATERNITY

THE THREE CONCEPTS OF LIBERTY, EQUALITY AND FRATERNITY MENTIONED IN THE PREAMBLE ARE TAKEN FROM THE CONSTITUTION OF FRANCE. THE FRENCH CONSTITUTION FOLLOWED THE FRENCH REVOLUTION IN 1789. THE FIRST WRITTEN CONSTITUTION WAS THAT OF THE UNITED STATES OF AMERICA.

Liberty

The Constitution says 'LIBERTY of thought, expression, belief, faith and worship'. Liberty is having freedom and to live in a state of being free from all kinds of restrictions and oppression. Liberty of thought means we can write and speak freely about what we think. This means most importantly that our press—newspapers, television and even social media, has the freedom of expression and that includes criticizing the people in power. Remember, the government has been elected by us and so, if it is criticized in the press that does not mean that the press is being 'anti-national'. A political party or the government is not the nation; we, the citizens, are the nation and they are our elected representatives for five years.

Liberty is also about our personal lives. Whatever we believe in, that is, in any political creed or religious faith, it is our right to do so, as long as it does not harm anyone else and it is not against the law. We have the liberty to live anywhere we like, choose any kind of work, make friends of our choice, marry whom we choose, eat and wear the things we like and travel anywhere in the country. As long as what we do is not against the law, we have been given the liberty to do so; even when people disapprove of what we do.

Equality

Then the Constitution talks of 'EQUALITY of status and of opportunity'. Equality means being of the same value and that is particularly important in Indian society, which is still very unequal and divided by caste.

It is a sad fact that Indians have always tended to separate and divide—by caste or varna, by tribe or jati, by religion and by a complex division called *gotra* that most of us can't even understand but obey blindly. Why do we do so? What do we gain from it? Whenever these divisions are pointed out to you, think of the rest of the world, they are doing fine without having jatis and gotras, then why are Indians still talking of ancient, outdated and unscientific social divisions that actually stop our progress? It really is a great mystery.

We judge people all the time as 'us and them'—by their class; that is as rich or poor; by caste, Brahmin, Shudra or Dalit; even by tribe as Jat or non Jat; by gender, male or female; and even by the colour of our skin. This would shock the founders of our nation, because they had fought against the caste system and for gender equality

for decades. According to the Constitution, no section of society can claim any special privilege unless it has been given by the Constitution, such as reservation for Scheduled Castes and Scheduled Tribes. The lower castes have gained some power over the years but the higher castes of Hindu society still deny equality to the Dalits. The battle for true equality still goes on.

Fraternity

Then, hoping for a peaceful and united nation, the Preamble talks of 'FRATERNITY assuring the dignity of the individual and the unity and integrity of the nation'. Fraternity is about a group of people sharing a common interest, offering friendship and mutual support. Our founders were hoping that in spite of all our many differences, we would find a way to live like brothers and sisters and most of the time, this does work—unless we start listening to people who want to divide us for their own selfish purposes.

So what the Preamble is saying very clearly is—this is the blueprint of our nation. Do not forget it and learn to think for yourself. Listen to everyone but make up your own mind. And a final word of warning comes from our first President Rajendra Prasad, he said our Constitution can be as good as the people who work it. So protect it; when you vote, choose your representative carefully and fight all those who are tempted to weaken it.

Never forget, you, as a citizen of India, are the most important person in the Constitution.

CHAPTER THREE

THE CONSTITUENT ASSEMBLY

'In the Assembly Indians were, for the first time in a century and a half, responsible for their own governance . . . A constitution, Assembly members realized, could not by itself make a new India, but they intended it to light the way.'

GRANVILLE AUSTIN

The setting up of a Constituent Assembly meant some very important things for Indians. It meant that after ruling India for nearly two centuries the British had finally decided to leave. Since 1885, the Congress Party has been demanding more power, saying that Indians had a right to rule themselves but their polite petitions had been ignored by the government with royal disdain. The attitude was that Indians were uneducated, uncivilized and lacked unity, so they could never govern themselves. The government was so confident about going on ruling India that they had even built a new capital city. New Delhi was inaugurated in 1931 as the capital of an empire that they arrogantly claimed would last a thousand years.

Then what changed seventeen years later? How did this miracle happen in 1947 that sent the British packing? And how was it that soon after, the magnificent Viceroy House was being renamed Rashtrapati Bhavan and an Indian freedom fighter, Chakravarty Rajagopalachari was taking over from the viceroy Lord Mountbatten as governor-general? And how were Indians proposing, debating and creating a constitution for themselves in the halls of the Parliament? The establishment of the Constituent Assembly sent out a message to Indians—soon, India was going to be free. So, to understand the creation of this very important organization called the Constituent Assembly, we need to go back in time and relive the exciting years of our freedom struggle.

The Call for *Azaadi*

So what had changed in the political landscape? The most important factor was of course our freedom movement. In the beginning, the Congress Party was an annual gathering of educated city men who did not really question the right of the British to rule India. The government was the 'mai baap sarkar', that is, it was like a benevolent parent who took care of their Indian subjects and we were happy to have an English Empress and, subsequently, her descendants as our monarchs. This obedient attitude began to change in the early years of the twentieth century with firebrand leaders like Bal Gangadhar Tilak and Lala Lajpat Rai, who began to talk of freedom. Tilak started the Swadeshi campaign in 1905 and suddenly, the mai baap sarkar was sending out the police and army to beat up peaceful protesters and the leaders were being shoved into prison. The fact that both Tilak and Lajpat Rai would be sent into solitary confinement in a jail in Burma shows that their campaign had been an effective one.

A hundred years ago, on 13 April 1919, on the day of Baisakhi, a horrific massacre took place at Jallianwala Bagh in Amritsar when General Dyer and his soldiers opened fire on a peaceful gathering of people and hundreds of men, women and children died. Dyer thought he was ending all political protest by Indians but instead, what he did was open the eyes of ordinary Indians to the reality of being a colonized people. When the First World War began in 1914, the government needed the cooperation of Indians and so, had promised them more power. But when the war ended, they went back on their word. Young Sikh soldiers had died on the battlefields of Europe for the British and now, Sikhs had been massacred in Amritsar where they had come to celebrate Baisakhi, their new year.

This fire lit at Jallianwalla Bagh grew into an all India movement that only wanted freedom. In 1915, a lawyer from South Africa returned to his homeland with some new ideas for a freedom movement. Mohandas Karamchand Gandhi called this strategy Satyagraha, the fight for truth. He combined it with Tilak's Swadeshi and welcomed the involvement of the common people, those who were willing to march out peacefully and face the police lathis and army guns and still sing of freedom.

Through the first decades of the twentieth century, the Congress led three major campaigns that were all

India movements—the Non-Cooperation Movement of 1920, the Civil Disobedience Movement of 1930 when Gandhiji began his headline-grabbing Dandi March and then the Quit India Movement of 1942, which went on despite the leadership being in jail because people did not stop protesting. For the government, this was a scary message. If the whole country went on strike, what would they do? Life in towns, cities and villages came to a halt; schools, colleges, law courts and offices were shut; and worse of all, no one would pay any taxes. Colonialism was ultimately about profits and with people on the march, India was not being profitable at all.

Events outside India also played a role in the British leaving their largest colony. Two world wars had meant that two generations of British young men had died on the battlefront and so, there were not enough men to join the Indian army or civil service to run a country that was becoming more and more rebellious. Suddenly, an Indian colony did not seem like such a good idea anymore. Soon, government commissions arrived to discuss the plan with Indian leaders like the Cripps Mission of 1942 and the Cabinet Mission of 1946. A lot of complicated talks followed, with M.A. Jinnah of the Muslim League disagreeing with everything suggested by the Congress and the Indian princes, maharajas and nawabs not being keen on democracy at all. Still, our leaders persisted and established the Constituent Assembly to lay down the foundation for a new democratic nation.

LET'S MEET

THE CONSTITUENT ASSEMBLY WAS FOUNDED ON 9 JULY 1946 AND FUNCTIONED FOR TWO YEARS, ELEVEN MONTHS AND EIGHTEEN DAYS. IT MET FOR THE FIRST TIME ON 9 DECEMBER 1946 AND ITS LAST SESSION WAS ON 24 JANUARY 1950. THE DAY WHEN THE CONSTITUTION WAS FORMALLY INAUGURATED WAS 26 JANUARY 1950—STILL CELEBRATED AS REPUBLIC DAY!

An Assembly Is Called

To write a complicated document like a Constitution, for a huge and complex country like India, needed a large group of highly qualified and experienced people. They won in an election and formed the Constituent Assembly.

As it became clear that India was going to be independent soon, the Assembly was elected in 1946 for the specific purpose of framing a constitution. At the time, India was divided into areas controlled by the government called British India and also many big and small Indian kingdoms ruled by rajas and nawabs called the princely states. These states were not independent at all of course. Their policies were controlled by the British who stationed a resident in their courts.

VOICES

ALBERT MAYER, AN AMERICAN ARCHITECT, DESCRIBED INDIAN LEADERS WITH THESE WORDS, 'THEIR ABILITY, OUTLOOK, ENERGY AND DEVOTION; THE TINGLING ATMOSPHERE OF PLANS AND EXPECTATIONS AND UNCERTAINTY; AND YET THE CALM AND SELF POSSESSION—WHAT IT ADDS UP TO IS BEING PRESENT AT THE BIRTH OF A NATION.'

The Assembly had 389 members, 296 from British India and 93 from the princely states. When India became independent in 1947, the Assembly also doubled as the first Parliament of the new nation till fresh elections were held from 1951 to 1952. As seats were only reserved for Muslims and Sikhs, the Congress Party made sure that other minority communities were represented within its members. Among the Congress members were Dalits, Parsis, Christians, tribal people, women and Anglo-Indians. Gandhiji recommended many eminent persons and so the Assembly members included many who were not even members of the party. However, don't think the election of 1946 (to elect members of the Constituent Assembly) was like our elections today. Most people were not allowed to vote. Still, it was an Indian assembly and its members had not been picked by the government.

The viceroy Lord Wavell was keen to play a leading role but he was politely told to stay away. Invitations were issued in the name of Sachchidanand Sinha, who was the oldest member of the Assembly, and not Wavell, underlining the fact that this was an Indian body. Later, Rajendra Prasad was elected as the permanent President. There were eight committees and the most crucial committee was the one that was called the Drafting Committee, which had the tough job of actually writing the Constitution. B.R. Ambedkar was made the Chairman of the Drafting Committee that presented a draft constitution that was published for public discussion and amendment before it was adopted.

From 1947 to 1949, India faced a baptism by fire. Even as the Assembly was meeting, there were the upheavals of the Partition and continuous communal violence across north India; there was an influx of crores upon crores of refugees who had to be housed and fed; Pakistan invaded Kashmir and this was soon followed by the tragic assassination of Mahatma Gandhi in January 1948. Through it all, the members fought on to formulate a constitution for a complex country with serious social and economic problems. Many of the members, such as

CHOOSING AMBEDKAR

B.R. AMBEDKAR WAS NOT A MEMBER OF THE
CONGRESS PARTY. FOR A LONG TIME, HE HAD
BEEN VERY CRITICAL OF GANDHIJI'S POLICIES,
ESPECIALLY ABOUT THE RIGHTS OF DALITS.
STILL, HIS NAME WAS PROPOSED BY GANDHIJI
AND ACCEPTED BY NEHRU BECAUSE HE WAS
BEST QUALIFIED TO LEAD THE DRAFTING
COMMITTEE AND FOR THE CONGRESS, A
MEMBER'S TALENTS WERE IMPORTANT NOT
HIS POLITICAL LOYALTIES.

Nehru, Patel and Azad, were at the same time, running the government. It is remarkable that the Constitution was ready in less than three years.

The Constituent Assembly had a lot on its platter. First, they had to create a government that would take care of all the social and economic problems. There was the abysmal poverty and the urgent need to improve agriculture so that we had enough food for everyone. Also, there was a need for roads and infrastructure, schools and hospitals, while at the same time, India had a deep lack of modern industrial development. Then, there were the social evils like the caste system and the oppression of the Dalits; the need for the emancipation of women, improving education and health care. National unity and security were also crucial issues.

If we achieved so much, it was because of the quality of the members. As historians noted, our leaders at the time knew how to work together, respect each other, discuss and even compromise. Historian Granville

Austin also observed, 'There is little if any evidence that caste considerations influenced Assembly members in the framing of the Constitution.'

WE TALKED A LOT

THE PROCEEDINGS OF THE CONSTITUENT ASSEMBLY FROM 1946 TO 1949 HAVE BEEN PRINTED IN TWELVE THICK VOLUMES CALLED CONSTITUENT ASSEMBLY DEBATES. SOME OF THESE VOLUMES HAVE MORE THAN A THOUSAND PAGES. IT SHOWS JUST HOW CAREFULLY EVERYTHING WAS DISCUSSED AND DEBATED AND ALSO THAT WE INDIANS DO LIKE TO TALK!

The atmosphere in the Assembly was very different from what we see in our Parliament today. If they could come back, people like Ambedkar, Patel and Azad would have been horrified by the shouting, disruptions and lack of cooperation in Parliament and the use of caste and religion as divisive factors. At the time, for the members of the Assembly, who were genuine patriots, their country came first, their political loyalties did not matter and they had work to do.

Problems Start Immediately

From day one, there were obstacles in the smooth running of the Assembly. In the elections, there were 296 seats assigned to the British Indian provinces. The Congress won 208 seats and the Muslim League got 73. Disappointed at not winning more seats, M.A. Jinnah, the leader of the Muslim League, immediately decided he would not cooperate with the Congress and demanded a separate assembly for Muslims. His claim was for a separate Muslim state called Pakistan. The new viceroy Lord Mountbatten then announced the Indian Independence Act of 1947, which created two nations— India and Pakistan. The Muslim League members then left the Constituent Assembly. India became independent on 15 August 1947 and now the membership was:

- The Congress: 208 seats
- Others: 15 seats
- Princely States: 93 seats

This Constituent Assembly of India met regularly for eleven sessions to draft a constitution that went into effect on 26 January 1950; the first elections were held in 1952 and we elected our first Parliament. Till then, the Assembly acted as the Indian Parliament.

Sessions of the Constituent Assembly

As you can make out from the list below, the Assembly worked very hard:

First Session: 9–23 December 1946
Second Session: 20–25 January 1947
Third Session: 28 April–2 May 1947
Fourth Session: 14–31 July 1947
Fifth Session: 14–30August 1947

MOMENTS TO REMEMBER

JAWAHARLAL NEHRU GAVE HIS MEMORABLE 'TRYST WITH DESTINY' SPEECH DURING THE FIFTH SESSION OF THE CONSTITUENT ASSEMBLY. THE CONSTITUTION WAS OFFICIALLY ADOPTED ON 26 NOVEMBER 1949. THE ASSEMBLY MET ON 24 JANUARY 1950 AND A COPY OF THE CONSTITUTION WAS SIGNED BY MEMBERS. IT CAME INTO FORCE ON 26 JANUARY 1950. AS THE STORY GOES, WHEN IT CAME TIME FOR THE MEMBERS TO SIGN THE CONSTITUTION, NEHRU WAS SO EXCITED THAT HE RUSHED TO SIGN AND DID NOT LEAVE ANY SPACE FOR RAJENDRA PRASAD WHOSE SIGNATURE, AS THE PRESIDENT OF THE ASSEMBLY, WOULD HAVE GONE ON TOP. SO PRASAD'S SIGNATURE IS SQUEEZED IN ON TOP OF NEHRU'S SIGNATURE AT AN ANGLE.

Sixth Session: 27 January 1948
Seventh Session: 4 November 1948–8 January 1949
Eighth Session: 16 May–16 June 1949
Ninth Session: 30 July–18 September 1949
Tenth Session: 6–17 October 1949
Eleventh Session: 14–26 November 1949

Many Subjects, Many Committees

The Constituent Assembly had to cover a wide range of subjects from the role of various departments of the government to the power of states to people's rights and duties. So thirteen committees were established and out of these, eight were major ones. These committees and their chairpersons were:

1. Drafting Committee (B.R. Ambedkar)
2. Union Powers Committee (Jawaharlal Nehru)
3. Union Constitution Committee (Jawaharlal Nehru)
4. Provincial Constitution Committee (Vallabhbhai Patel)
5. Advisory Committee on Fundamental Rights, Minorities and tribal and Excluded Areas (Vallabhbhai Patel)
   This important committee had to handle very complex topics and so it had to be divided into four sub committees:

   - Fundamental Rights Sub Committee, headed by J.B. Kripalani
   - Minorities Sub Committee, headed by Harendra Coomar Mookerjee

- North-East Frontier Tribal Areas and Assam Excluded & partially Excluded Areas Sub Committee, headed by Gopinath Bordoloi
- Excluded and partially Excluded Areas (Other than those in Assam), headed by A.V. Thakkar

6. Rules of Procedure Committee (Rajendra Prasad)
7. States Committee (Committee for Negotiating with States) (Jawaharlal Nehru)
8. Steering Committee (Rajendra Prasad)

The Drafting Committee

The members of the crucial Drafting Committee included: B.R. Ambedkar as Chairman, and B.L. Mitter, N.G. Ayyangar, A.K. Ayyar, K.M. Munshi, Mohammad Saadulla, N. Madhava Rau, D.P. Khaitan, T.T. Krishnamachari.

Fundamental Rights Subcommittee

The subcommittee on Fundamental Rights worked on the crucial topic of the rights of the people. Its members were: J.B. Kripalani, Chairman. M.R. Masani. K.T. Shah. Rajkumari Amrit Kaur, Mrs Hansa Mehta, A.K. Ayyar, K.M. Munshi, Harnam Singh, Maulana Abul Kalam Azad, B.R. Ambedkar, Jairamdas Daulatram, K.N. Panikker.

What Happened at These Sessions?

It was a very well-organized system. The various committees discussed their assigned subjects and came up with their proposals, which were presented to the Assembly. Once the Assembly had debated and finalized the report, it was handed over to the Constitutional Adviser B.N. Rau. He was an expert on constitutions and he prepared an initial draft in the correct legal language for the Drafting Committee. Finally, the Drafting Committee, chaired by Ambedkar, presented a detailed draft constitution that was published for public discussion. This draft constitution was then discussed, amended and passed by the Assembly. This meant that every member had the opportunity to suggest and comment on any report.

PROMINENT WOMEN

MANY WOMEN STOOD FOR ELECTIONS, WON AND BECAME MEMBERS OF THE CONSTITUENT ASSEMBLY.

THESE MEMBERS WERE: AMMU SWAMINATHAN (MADRAS), ANNIE MASCARENE (TRAVANCORE & COCHIN), BEGUM AIZAZ RAZUL (UNITED PROVINCES), DAKSHAYANI VELUYUDAN (MADRAS), G. DURGABAI DESHMUKH (MADRAS), HANSA MEHTA (BOMBAY), PURNIMA BANERJEE (UNITED PROVINCES), RENUKA ROY (WEST BENGAL), SAROJINI NAIDU (BIHAR), SUCHETA KRIPALANI (UNITED PROVINCES), VIJAYA LAKSHMI PANDIT (UNITED PROVINCES), KAMALA CHAUDHURI (UNITED PROVINCES), RAJKUMARI AMRIT KAUR (CENTRAL PROVINCES)

MANY HAD OTHER OFFICIAL ROLES TOO, SUCH AS RAJKUMARI AMRIT KAUR, WHO WAS IN THE CABINET OF THE CENTRAL GOVERNMENT AS THE MINISTER OF HEALTH AND SAROJINI NAIDU, WHO WOULD BECOME THE GOVERNOR OF THE UNITED PROVINCES. THE PRINCELY STATES DID NOT NOMINATE ANY WOMEN.

Much More than a Constitution

When the Assembly met for the first time on 9 December 1946, in his inimitable style, Jawaharlal Nehru put into words what he hoped the constitution would achieve, 'The first task of this Assembly is to free India through a new constitution, to feed the starving people, and to clothe the naked masses, and to give every Indian the fullest opportunity to develop himself according to his capacity.' Then he warned, 'But at present, the greatest and most important question in India is how to solve the problem of the poor and the starving. Wherever we turn, we are confronted with this problem. If we cannot solve this problem soon, all our paper constitutions will become useless and purposeless.'

So the constitution was not just going to be a carefully worded legal document about how the government was to be run but also took up the challenge of improving the lives of the Indian people. It was as much a social and an economic document.

> ## VOICES
>
> 'CONSTITUTIONAL MORALITY IS NOT A NATURAL SENTIMENT. IT HAS TO BE CULTIVATED. WE MUST REALIZE THAT OUR PEOPLE HAVE YET TO LEARN IT. DEMOCRACY IN INDIA IS ONLY A TOP-DRESSING ON AN INDIAN SOIL, WHICH IS ESSENTIALLY UNDEMOCRATIC.'— B.R. AMBEDKAR

Creating an Outline of the Constitution

The work was done in a very careful and organized manner because the constitution of a country is too important to be taken lightly. First, there were experts on the many constitutions of the world that were studied, like those of the United Kingdom, United States, the Soviet Republic, France and Ireland. The features that were felt to be suitable for India were discussed and among the features adopted from other constitutions were the parliamentary system of Britain instead of the presidential system of the USA. The crucial Fundamental Rights were inspired by the American constitution. The Fundamental Duties were taken from the USSR and Directive Principles from Ireland.

Then the Constitution was carefully divided into different parts and each part was further divided into Articles. For instance, Part II deals with Citizenship and Part III with Fundamental Rights. Then Part VI deals with the States, Part XIII with Trade, Commerce and

Intercourse within the Territory of India and Part XV with Elections. Within the 395 Articles and 8 Schedules, the Assembly was doing its best to make every function of the government clear, while at the same time, trying to anticipate newer challenges in the future. It was not an easy job and the fact that so many years later, in 2020, the Constitution still does not feel out of date but is, in fact, relevant to our lives today says something about how hard the members of the Assembly worked.

CHAPTER FOUR

LEADERS OF THE CONSTITUENT ASSEMBLY

'What are we having this liberty for? We are having this liberty in order to reform our social system which is so full of inequities, discrimination and other things which conflict with our fundamental rights.'

B.R. AMBEDKAR

The Constitution of India was the creation of many minds; of people of different streams of political thought and also of both men and women. What was important was that it was a creation exclusively by Indians; no one was dictating any clause to us. We studied the many constitutions in use across the world, selected items that we felt were relevant to India and then debated, changed and drafted the ideas.

THE JAPANESE CONSTITUTION

JUST AFTER THE SECOND WORLD WAR, JAPAN GOT A CONSTITUTION BUT IT HAD LITTLE TO DO WITH THE WISHES OF THE JAPANESE PEOPLE. THIS WAS THE TIME WHEN JAPAN WAS OCCUPIED BY THE UNITED STATES AFTER ITS DEFEAT IN THE WAR. THE AMERICANS DRAFTED A CONSTITUTION AND IT WAS PRESENTED TO THE JAPANESE PEOPLE. THE BRITISH WOULD HAVE LIKED TO DO THE SAME IN INDIA BUT THE CONSTITUENT ASSEMBLY STOOD FIRM.

With the formation of the various committees, a small group of about twenty members emerged as a core group that played a crucial role in the actual framing of the constitution. They were all national heroes and heroines, who had played stellar roles in the freedom movement and their stature added both prestige and experience to the proceedings, which saw many passionate debates. There were many opinions that were expressed on the floor of the Assembly but the debates were always held in a democratic and civilized manner. No one yelled, threw a tantrum or invaded the well of the Assembly where the Speaker sat. Many of these stalwarts have been forgotten and we need to remember them as we celebrate the many decades of having the constitution. They all made very valuable contributions with their ideas.

The six most active and influential members of the Assembly were Jawaharlal Nehru, Sardar Patel, B.R. Ambedkar, Maulana Azad, Sarojini Naidu and Rajendra Prasad. All highly educated and experienced leaders who had given much thought to the forming of the constitution. Govind Ballabh Pant, Rajkumari Amrit Kaur, Hansa Mehta, Durgabai Deshmukh, Pattabhi Sitaramayya, Alladi Krishnaswamy Ayyar, N.G. Ayyangar, K.M. Munshi and Satyanarayan Sinha were some of the other prominent members.

As Bipan Chandra writes, 'They brought diverse backgrounds, personalities and qualifications to constitution making.' They were all university graduates, some like Nehru, Ambedkar and Patel were lawyers who had earned their degrees abroad and Ambedkar possessed one of the most formidable legal minds in the Assembly. Besides lawyers, the Assembly also had doctors, teachers and bureaucrats among its members. In spite of the Congress being the dominant party, many like Ambedkar, Begum Aizaz, Rasuland Shyama and Prasad Mukherjee were not Congress members.

What added both knowledge and relevance to the deliberation of the various committees was that some of the members were also part of the government that was struggling with extraordinarily complex problems—there were refugees to be rehabilitated; severe food shortages; and law and order problems with communal riots flaring up all across north India. The reality of the political and social situation outside the walls of the Assembly affected the work of framing the constitution.

If the constitution is, in many ways, a revolutionary document striving to create justice and equality, and achieve social and economic progress, it is because of the circumstances in which it was created and the people who framed it.

So let us learn about this team that gave us the road map to the future—a people's document—the Constitution of India. They make a fascinating collage of portraits. The story of their lives makes for very interesting reading.

B.R. Ambedkar

Often called the architect of the Constitution, Bhimrao Ramji Ambedkar was born on 14 April 1891 in Mhow in Central India. He was the fourteenth and last child of Ramji Sakpal and Bhimabai and belonged to the Mahar caste that was considered an 'untouchable' by the caste ridden Hindu society. The Mahars had a martial history, they had fought in the army of Shivaji, and Ramji Sakpal had served in the Indian army. This meant that he could educate his children even though he had very little money.

Bhimrao's first day in school taught him the bitter reality about what it was to be a member of the oppressed classes in Hindu India. He and his brother had to sit outside the class on gunny sacks that they carried from home, and the teachers ignored them. The other children did not play with them and never shared their food. Even to get some drinking water, they had to wait next to the well till someone was kind enough to pour water into

HOW CAN A HUMAN BEING BE UNTOUCHABLE?

HINDU SOCIETY IS THE ONLY ONE IN THE WORLD THAT DIVIDES SOCIETY INTO WHAT IS CALLED VARNA OR JATI, USUALLY CALLED CASTE IN ENGLISH. THE WORLD GOES ON JUST FINE WITHOUT A CASTE SYSTEM, BUT HINDUS HOLD ON TO IT WITHOUT ANY LOGIC OR HUMANITY. IT IS WIDELY CONSIDERED TO BE AMONG THE WORST RACIST SYSTEMS IN THE WORLD, RIGHT NEXT TO SOUTH AFRICA'S APARTHEID.

IT IS A VERY CONFUSING SYSTEM WITH SO MANY JATIS THAT IT IS HARD TO KEEP COUNT! PRIMARILY, IT PUSHES OUT WHAT THE BRAHMANS AND KSHATRIYAS CALL 'LOWER' CASTES, SO THAT THEY CAN HOLD ON TO POWER AND MONEY. WE STRUGGLE TO GIVE THEM A NAME THAT DOES NOT INSULT THEIR HUMANITY. MANY WORDS HAVE BEEN USED— LOWER, OPPRESSED, OUTCASTE, SCHEDULED CASTES, UNTOUCHABLE OR WHAT GANDHIJI CALLED THEM, HARIJANS.

IN THIS BOOK, WE HAVE CHOSEN TO REFER TO THEM AS DALITS, WHICH SIMPLY MEANS OPPRESSED BECAUSE THAT IS WHAT MODERN MEMBERS OF THIS SOCIETY LIKE TO CALL THEMSELVES. DECADES AFTER THE INAUGURATION OF THE CONSTITUTION, THE DALITS ARE STILL BATTLING FOR THEIR RIGHTS AGAINST THE UPPER CASTESAND AMBEDKAR'S PROUD SPIRIT HOVERS OVER THEM.

their waiting hands. This was usually a peon and if he was not around, they remained thirsty till they got back home.

Young Bhimrao never forgot this experience and dedicated his life to fighting for the rights of the Dalits with a single-minded passion and a defiant rage. In Ambedkar, the downtrodden Dalits finally found a courageous, tough talking, formidably knowledgeable and energetic leader who would demand and win them self-respect and equality. For all the young Dalits, he became a role model because he put his heart and soul into giving them equality within the Constitution, which finally made the loathsome Hindu caste system illegal.

One day, this boy who was being denied an education was given a scholarship by Sayajirao Gaekwad III, the reformist ruler of the kingdom of Baroda, to study abroad. Ambedkar went on to earn a PhD from Columbia University, a Master's degree and later a doctorate from the London School of Economics. At the same time, he gained a law degree from Gray's Inn and become a barrister. So ultimately, he had four doctorates and a law degree! Once he was back in India, he realized that despite his achievements, people's behaviour towards him hadn't changed. He was to work in Baroda but could not do so because no one would rent him a room and people at his office would throw files on to his table from a distance to avoid touching him. Later, when he worked as a lecturer in a Bombay college, his colleagues refused to drink from the same jug of water. Finally, he chose to become a lawyer and began a campaign to help Dalits. As he said, 'The outcaste is a by-product of the caste system. There will be outcastes as long as there are castes. Nothing can emancipate the outcaste except the destruction of the caste system.'

Ambedkar began a satyagraha against Dalits being stopped from entering temples and he led a group of protestors to the Chavdar Taley, a public water tank from which Dalits were not allowed to take water. Ambedkar and his followers drank the water and then burnt a copy of Manusmriti, the ancient Sanskrit treatise which is believed to be the source of all inequality in Hindu society. Ambedkar showed how it supported the caste system and how it was against gender equality. He had studied Hindu scriptures so deeply he could demolish any arguments by Hindu pundits trying to defend the caste system. While practising law in Bombay, Ambedkar began helping Dalits get educated by setting up schools, colleges, hostels, libraries and study circles. He became an inspiration to Dalits, who now began to question their social status in Hindu society; their affectionate name for him was Babasaheb, respected father.

BABASAHEB AND BOOKS

WHEN HE WAS RETURNING TO INDIA FROM LONDON, AMBEDKAR HAD TO SEND HIS HUGE COLLECTION OF BOOKS BY A SEPARATE SHIP AND THAT SHIP SANK. LATER WHEN HE BUILT A HOUSE, HE HAD A LIBRARY THAT HOUSED ABOUT 50,000 BOOKS. HE ALWAYS BELIEVED THAT IT WAS EDUCATION THAT WOULD BE THE SALVATION OF DALITS.

In the Constituent Assembly, with his great scholarship in jurisprudence and constitutional law, Ambedkar was the most qualified and the perfect choice to head the Drafting Committee. He had studied the constitutions of many countries and was the best suited to draft the constitution. In the Assembly debates, he raised his voice to fight for the rights of not just the Dalits but also women. He was the first Law Minister of India, and introduced reservations for Dalits in education and government jobs. This was similar to the affirmative action that was started in the United States of America to help the African Americans who were the descendants of former slaves.

For a long time, Ambedkar had been seeking a religion that offered equality to all and found it in the teachings of the Buddha. He converted to Buddhism in 1956 and as many Dalits followed, it led to a revival of Buddhism in the country. He once said, 'Unfortunately for me, I was born a Hindu Untouchable. It was beyond my power to prevent that, but I declare that I will not die a Hindu.' Ambedkar died the same year and a stupa has been built at the site of his cremation in Dadar in Maharashtra called Chaitanya Bhumi and it has become a pilgrimage for Dalits.

Ambedkar was awarded the Bharat Ratna posthumously only in 1990; the delay would not have surprised him. His greatest legacy is that in today's India, the Dalits have gained the courage to stand up, protest and demand their legal rights. It is because Ambedkar made sure that they got equality and respect from the Constitution. He was a knowledgeable jurist, thoughtful economist, compassionate social reformer, an honest and hard-working politician and most importantly, the conscience of the Assembly; the people of India have never forgotten him.

Jawaharlal Nehru

You couldn't have a greater contrast than the lives of B.R. Ambedkar and Jawaharlal Nehru. Born on 14 November 1889 in Allahabad, Jawaharlal was the eldest child of Motilal Nehru and Swarup Rani. Since Motilal was the most successful lawyer in the city, he grew up in great luxury. The Nehrus lived in a mansion, owned the first car in the city, had a swimming pool and a tennis court; young Jawaharlal even had a pony! He could have easily remained the pampered son of a wealthy family and floated through life; instead, he chose to join the freedom movement, faced the lathis of the police and was in fact imprisoned for a longer period that even Gandhiji and Sardar Patel. Both true patriots, Ambedkar and Nehru respected each other and worked with extraordinary cooperation to create a remarkable document. They were a perfect balance of realistic and visionary, as the meticulous drafting and clear purpose came from the practical and knowledgeable Ambedkar and the soaring dreams and aspirations from Nehru. More than anyone else, we owe the constitution to these two towering personalities.

Nehru was sent off to England to study at the exclusive school of Harrow where Indian princes studied and then went to Trinity College in Cambridge and also joined the Bar at Inner Temple but unlike Ambedkar, he displayed little academic brilliance. As his biographer, Sarvepalli Gopal writes, when he returned to India, 'Jawaharlal had opinions but needed a cause; there stretched before him a future secure but with no purpose.' He attended the first Congress session in 1912 and was not impressed by the gathering of the very *pucca* sahib delegates, who seemed to be out of touch with the realities of India. He discovered his path after the massacre at Jallianwala Bagh and his first meeting with Mahatma Gandhi. His faith in the justice of the British government was broken when he found that General Dyer, who had ordered the firing, was never punished.

Nehru met Gandhiji in 1916 and found the leader and mentor he would follow for the rest of his life. It was a fascinating relationship between a religious, traditional, economically conservative Mahatma and a modern, agnostic, socialist Nehru. They often argued, there were times when Gandhiji made him so angry that he would walk out of a meeting and pace outside to calm himself; but they remained close because their chosen path was the same and they both made extraordinary sacrifices for their cause. They were part of a much larger picture where they had to struggle to win freedom and at the end, it was Nehru that Gandhi anointed as his successor.

GANDHI ON NEHRU

THERE IS A LOVELY PHOTOGRAPH OF GANDHIJI, NEHRU AND PATEL WHERE GANDHIJI IS SITTING IN THE MIDDLE, TALKING AWAY, WITH THE OTHER TWO LEANING IN TOWARDS HIM LIKE AFFECTIONATE SONS. THE THREE SHARED A VERY SPECIAL BOND THAT WAS A BLEND OF ADMIRATION, TRUST AND LOVE; SOMETHING THAT IS VERY RARE IN POLITICS. GANDHIJI KNEW THAT MANY PEOPLE WERE PUZZLED BY THE CLOSENESS BETWEEN NEHRU AND HIM AND TRIED TO EXPLAIN THIS COMPLEX RELATIONSHIP, 'IT WILL REQUIRE MUCH MORE THAN DIFFERENCE OF OPINION TO ESTRANGE US . . . HE SAYS THAT HE DOES NOT UNDERSTAND MY LANGUAGE, AND THAT HE SPEAKS A LANGUAGE FOREIGN TO ME . . . BUT LANGUAGE IS NO BAR TO A UNION OF HEARTS. AND I KNOW THIS, THAT WHEN I AM GONE, HE WILL SPEAK MY LANGUAGE.'

Nehru would be part of every mass movement led by Gandhiji—the Non-Cooperation Movement of 1920; the Civil Disobedience Movement of 1930 and the Quit India Movement of 1942. He travelled all across India, spoke to thousands of people and gained first-hand knowledge of the lives of Indians as he walked from village to village. He wrote of his encounter with India's common folk, 'A new picture of India seemed to rise before me, naked, starving, crushed and utterly miserable.' He put in many years of thought into what the Indian Constitution should achieve to improve the lives of the poorest Indian and it came from this experience.

A charismatic speaker and popular writer in newspapers, he was soon among the Congress Party's key orators and his charm and empathy for common people made him hugely popular. Soon, his father Motilal and the whole Nehru clan had joined the freedom struggle, everyone nattily clad in khadi clothes. When he was elected the President of the Congress Party in 1929, he declared that the aim was to gain Purna Swaraj, i.e., total independence. On 26 January 1930, he unfurled the tricolour flag at Lahore by the banks of the River Ravi and declared 26 January as Independence Day. Today, we celebrate it as our Republic Day.

The government often avoided arresting Gandhiji, fearing protests; so they targeted Nehru instead, who would spend a total of over eleven years in jail, often in solitary confinement, living in dark, rat-infested cells that were unbearably hot in summer and cold in winter and eating awful prison food. Here, he began to write books, mainly for his daughter Indira. *Glimpses of World History* and the magnificent *A Discovery of*

India are books that are still read and referenced today. He was not always allowed to get books and was often writing from his prodigious memory. What is even more amazing is that there is no bitterness or anger in his words, instead, a lyrical elegance permeates his style, 'The moon, ever a companion to me in prison, has grown more friendly with closer acquaintance, a reminder of the loveliness of this world . . . Ever changing, yet ever the same . . .'

INDIA CAN PROSPER ONLY WHEN POOR INDIANS PROSPER.

When India became independent on 15 August 1947, Jawaharlal Nehru was sworn in as the first Prime Minister of the country in the Constituent Assembly. His magnificent speech, which spoke of India's tryst with destiny, has never been forgotten and continues to inspire us. Soon he would be back in the Assembly, helping to write India's Constitution, which for him was not just a legal document but also a treatise on the social and economic state of India. He did not rise from the poor but he had the greatest empathy for the life and struggles of peasants. More than anyone else in the Assembly, he recognized that the fight was an economic one and that the only way poor Indians could prosper was if they made it the foundation of the constitution.

Jawaharlal Nehru's love for the land and its people was deep and abiding, and for him, Bharat Mata was not just the land but all its people—of every religion, every region, men, women and children. People sensed this and gave back a love and trust nearly as deep as the one they gave to Mahatma Gandhi. We say that Gandhiji led the movement that gave us freedom. If so, Ambedkar and Nehru gave us a future as an independent country through the Constitution of India.

Abul Kalam Azad

Abul Kalam means 'Lord of the dialogue'; he was a brilliant orator and talented at debates. He was a childhood prodigy who spoke six languages and began giving scholarly lectures when he was just fifteen years old. Abul Kalam Azad was among the most trusted members of the Congress Party, always part of the group taking important decisions, leading protests and going to jail. He was also a scholar, poet and journalist and was very popular for his masterful oratory. Like Gandhiji, he was against the partition of the country and for this, he faced insults from the Muslim League and Jinnah, who called him a traitor to the cause of Pakistan. For Azad, secularism and the unity of India came together.

Azad was born on 11 November 1888 in Mecca, to an Indian father and an Arab mother. His father had settled in Mecca after the Uprising of 1857 but soon returned to Calcutta where Azad grew up. His father was a famous scholar of Islamic studies and young Abul Kalam was a prodigy who quickly gained the title of Maulana. He was expected to be an Islamic teacher but he started a newspaper and was soon part of the rough and tumble of the freedom movement, joining the Congress in 1920. He was thrown in jail several times and was part of the team that negotiated with the British Government to gain independence.

Azad was the first Minister of Education, Culture and Fine Arts of Independent India and established many educational and cultural institutions like the University Grants Commission, Sangeet Natak Akademi and the Sahitya Akademi. He also established the first Indian Institute of Technology at Kharagpur and, along with Ajmal Khan, founded the Jamia Millia Islamia University in Delhi.

BEHIND PRISON WALLS

AZAD WAS FIRST PUT IN JAIL FOR HIS WRITING
IN HIS URDU NEWSPAPER AL HILAL, WHICH
CHAMPIONED INDIA'S FREEDOM FIGHTERS.
IN 1942, DURING THE QUIT INDIA MOVEMENT,
HE, NEHRU AND PATEL WERE IMPRISONED
IN AHMEDNAGAR FORT AND HE WROTE TO
A FRIEND, 'ONLY NINE MONTHS EARLIER . . .
THE GATE OF NAINI CENTRAL JAIL WAS
OPENED BEFORE ME . . . AND YESTERDAY
THE NEW GATE OF THE AHMEDNAGAR FORT
WAS CLOSED BEHIND ME.' HE SPENT A TOTAL
OF TEN YEARS AND FIVE MONTHS IN PRISON
DURING HIS LIFETIME, BATTLING HIS POOR
HEALTH THAT WORSENED IN JAIL.

With the other Muslim leaders like M.A. Ansari, Asaf Ali, Rafi Ahmed Kidwai and Ghaffar Khan, Azad left an inspiring legacy of Hindu–Muslim harmony. He was the President of the Congress twice and led the delegation in negotiations with the various government committees set up to prepare for India's independence. Nehru appreciated his sharp mind and ability to negotiate and called him Mir-i-Karawan, or the leader of the caravan, and his debating skills were often appreciated in the Assembly. In the Constituent Assembly, Azad was a member of a number of committees and spoke on a number of subjects including the state of the minorities in India and the importance of communal harmony for India's progress. Azad died in 1958 and he was awarded the Bharat Ratna in 1992.

Rajendra Prasad

In 1917, Mahatma Gandhi arrived in Champaran in Bihar to fight for the rights of the indigo farmers who were being exploited by English planters. Arriving at Patna, he stayed at the home of a young lawyer named Rajendra Prasad who immediately joined his campaign, travelled to Champaran and for the rest of his life, never left Gandhiji's side. Rajendra Prasad was a part of every major campaign initiated by Gandhiji and worked to build an efficient party. One day he would be elected unanimously as the President of the Constituent Assembly and would go on to become the first President of India. Rajendra Prasad was awarded the Bharat Ratna in 1962.

Prasad was born on 3 December 1884 in the village of Zeradei in Bihar and attended the Chhapra Zilla School. He completed his Master's degree from Calcutta University and then studied law and practiced at Calcutta High Court and then at Patna High Court. These were the days of the agitation against the partition of Bengal by Lord Curzon and he joined the protest movement. The meeting with Gandhiji was a turning point in his life and like many other young men, he wholeheartedly dedicated his life to the freedom struggle.

BE INDIAN

WHEN HE BECAME PRESIDENT OF INDIA, RAJENDRA PRASAD ENTERED THE RASHTRAPATI BHAWAN WHICH WAS A VERY WESTERNIZED ESTABLISHMENT WITH BUTLERS AND VALETS; FORMAL DINNERS WITH A EUROPEAN MENU AND EVENING TEA SERVED WITH CAKES AND SCONES. HE SOON CHANGED IT TO THE HOME OF AN INDIAN PRESIDENT. WE HAVE A PHOTOGRAPH, FOUND IN OLD ARCHIVES, OF A FORMAL DINNER WHERE HE AND HIS GUESTS ARE EATING ON BRASS THALIS AND WITH THE FOOD SERVED IN *KATORIS*. SADLY, NO ONE REMEMBERS WHAT THE MENU WAS!

Rajendra Prasad was an efficient and organized President of the Constituent Assembly, always ensuring that there was decorum even during some very angry debates and he also ensured that members of every hue of opinions were allowed to present their case. All the drafts were circulated among the members well in advance so that they could study them and in this way, he ensured that the work of the Assembly moved smoothly. He was also the chairman of a number of committees including the crucial Steering Committee and Finance Committee and spoke about the rights of the minorities. After serving as President of India for two terms, Rajendra Prasad died in 1963.

Vallabhbhai Patel

In 1915, when Vallabhbhai Patel and his friends, all successful men, were playing bridge at the Gujarat Club in Ahmedabad, a thin man wearing the clothes of a peasant, a dhoti, kurta and a huge wobbly turban, came up to them and requested that they come and listen to Mahatma Gandhi's lecture. This was the first time Vallabhbhai Patel met Gandhiji and he was not impressed at all! But soon, the two men would become brothers in arms in our freedom struggle and Gandhiji would teach Sanskrit to his friend in Yerawada Jail.

Vallabhbhai Patel was born on 31 October 1875 in Nadiad, Gujarat. His grandfather had fought in the army of Laxmi Bai, the rani of Jhansi during the Uprising of 1857, so patriotism was not a new concept to him. He and his older brother Vithalbhai both joined the freedom movement. Patel got a barrister's degree from Middle Temple in London. He would walk ten miles every day to save the bus fare and yet, topped his class. After meeting Gandhiji, he gave up his successful law practice, threw his suits and hats in a bonfire and began wearing a khadi dhoti and kurta.

Gandhiji had come from South Africa after a campaign fighting for the rights of the Indian community against the ruthless apartheid of the white regime. He did not know if his strategy of non-violent protests, that he called Satyagraha, would work in India. He and Patel organized two farmers' agitations in Gujarat's Kheda and Bardoli districts.

The farmers were demanding lowering of taxes but the government had refused. So Satyagraha meant that the farmers refused to pay any tax. Patel moved into the area, living in villages and standing beside the people against the police and tax collectors. Land, crops, cattle and even ploughs were seized; farmers were arrested but they held firm because they knew that their demands were justified. Most importantly, it was a completely peaceful agitation and the government had to yield because soon the protests began to spread. It was the women of Bardoli who began calling Patel 'Sardar' and he carried the title with great pride for the rest of his life.

Through all the following years of campaigns—the movements of Non-cooperation, Civil Disobedience and Quit India—it was Patel who was Gandhiji's right hand man. He expertly organized the Congress Party and the India-wide campaigns of boycotts and demonstrations. At a time when there were only postcards and telephones, no email or mobile phones, he had people marching out together in every corner of India. He was the fundraiser and tough party boss, known for his ruthless efficiency—it earned him his second title, 'Iron Man of India'.

During the last years of the British rule, through all the complex negotiations before India could become independent, the team from the Congress was made up of Nehru, Patel and Azad. During the negotiations around the partition of the country, he fought hard to keep the regions that had a Hindu majority in India. Jinnah had imperiously demanded all of Bengal and Punjab for Pakistan but he had to be satisfied with a much smaller area.

Patel's greatest contribution to Independent India was as the deputy Prime Minister and Minister for States. The India that we know today exists because of Patel. In 1947, there were over five-hundred princely states dotted across the map, some were large provinces like Hyderabad and Kashmir and others just a cluster of villages with a small-time raja. The problem was that these states were all independent and had to be legally brought into the Indian Union. So, the princes had to sign an Instrument of Accession and Patel made sure every single one of them did so; some by persuasion and others by the threat of military action. If, today, India does not have a single kingdom and is a democracy, it is because of the hard work of Patel.

In the Constituent Assembly, Patel headed a number of important committees and spoke often. Ramachandra Guha writes, 'The bulk of the back room work was done by Vallabhbhai Patel. A consummate committee man, he played a key role in the drafting of the various reports. It was Patel, rather than the less patient Nehru, who worked at mediating between warring groups, taking recalcitrant members with him on his morning walks and making them see the larger point of view.' Patel was deeply affected by the assassination of Gandhiji in 1948. His health was already fragile and now it began to deteriorate further and he died in 1950.

Sarojini Naidu

During the Civil Disobedience movement of 1930, the most headline-grabbing Satyagraha was led by a woman. Gandhiji's famous march to Dandi had galvanized the nation and he was subsequently arrested. It was now up to the other leaders to carry on with the protest against the salt tax. On 21 May 1930, on a blisteringly hot summer day, freedom fighters gathered outside the Dharasana Salt Works at Gujarat. They were led by Sarojini Naidu, the first Indian woman President of the Indian National Congress.

The salt works had been surrounded by barbed wire as policemen armed with rifles and steel-tipped lathis stood guard. Naidu reminded the freedom fighters that their demonstrations had to be absolutely peaceful, 'You will be beaten, but you must not resist,' she said. 'You must not even raise a hand to ward off blows.' What followed was an example of extraordinary courage as groups of marchers walked up to the gate of the salt works and faced a barrage of lathi blows. Women volunteers ran to help the injured and bandaged their wounds even as another group began to walk. As newspapers across the world reported the horrifying scene, 320 freedom fighters were injured and two were killed but no protestor had picked up a stone or fought back. Dharasana revealed the real face of the British Raj and the support for our struggle grew across the world.

Sarojini Chattopadhyay was born in Hyderabad on 13 February 1879 to Aghorenath and Baradasundari Chattopadhyay. Her father was a scientist and established the Nizam's College and supported the education of

80

women. Young Sarojini was a prodigy who showed a talent for poetry and had completed her schooling at the age of twelve. The Nizam offered her a scholarship and she studied at King's College, London and then Girton College, Cambridge.

She published a number of poetry collections and at the age of nineteen, she married Muthyala Govindarajulu Naidu, a military doctor. Her marriage created quite a stir as she chose her husband who was not only a south Indian from Hyderabad, but also of a lower caste. So she was an independent woman who not only ignored the caste barrier but also the one of region and language.

SUBHADRA SEN GUPTA

FIRST MEETING

SAROJINI NAIDU AND GANDHIJI SHARED A VERY
SPECIAL RELATIONSHIP. SHE MET HIM IN 1914
AND DESCRIBED HER FIRST SIGHT OF THE
'LITTLE MAN' WITH TYPICAL HUMOUR. SHE
SAW A MAN WITH SHAVEN HEAD, SITTING
ON THE FLOOR ON A BLACK PRISON BLANKET
EATING SQUASHED TOMATOES AND OLIVE OIL
OUT OF A WOODEN BOWL. SHE HAD LAUGHED
AT THE AMUSING PICTURE PRESENTED BY A
FAMOUS LEADER AND FROM THAT MOMENT,
THEY SHARED A VERY SPECIAL BOND. SHE
WOULD OFTEN TEASE HIM, AND HE WOULD
ENJOY HER IRREVERENT COMMENTS. ONLY
NAIDU COULD GET AWAY WITH CALLING A
SENIOR LEADER LIKE GANDHIJI 'MICKEY MOUSE'
BECAUSE OF HIS LARGE EARS!

Naidu was a brilliant orator and thousands would gather to listen to her mesmerizing speeches. In a sea of white khadi, she was often the centre of attention as a glamorous figure in gorgeous silk saris. She inspired women, students and factory workers to join the freedom movement and took her message abroad. She led a whirlwind tour of the United States where her speeches were followed by standing ovations. Naidu became an inspiration for Indian women and many stepped out of their homes, breaking the purdah to become educated and fight for their rights.

Among the women members of the Constituent Assembly, she was the tallest figure, wielding much influence. After Independence, Nehru appointed her the Governor of the largest state of United Provinces (modern Uttar Pradesh). Gandhiji's death was a devastating shock for Naidu who called him her 'friend and master' and said, 'This was the only death great enough for him . . . time is over for personal sorrow . . . The time is here and now when we stand up and say, "We take up the challenge" to those who defied Mahatma Gandhi.' Naidu died soon after on 2 March 1949 and the poet's lyrical voice fell silent forever.

Speaking Up for Women

The Constituent Assembly had fifteen women members, belonging to different regions of the country and with very different social backgrounds. All of them were educated, independent and courageous people who stood up and spoke in the Assembly, often disagreeing with the male members who did not want to take them seriously.

These women members were: Ammu Swaminathan, Dakshayani Velayudhan, Begum Aizaz Rasul, Durgabai Deshmukh, Hansa Jivraj Mehta, Kamla Chaudhri, Leela Roy, Malati Choudhury, Purnima Banerjee, Rajkumari Amrit Kaur, Renuka Ray, Sarojini Naidu, Sucheta Kripalani, Vijaya Lakshmi Pandit and Annie Mascarene.

Each of them has an inspiring story to tell. Ammu Swaminathan, for example, spoke in the Constituent Assembly and later in the Lok Sabha and Rajya Sabha, about the emancipation and equal rights for women. Many patriarchal members had declared in the Assembly that all women did not deserve the right to vote. Swaminathan said in reply, 'People outside have been saying that India did not give equal rights to her women. Now we can say that when the Indian people themselves framed their constitution, they have given rights to women equal with every other citizen of the country.'

Another important Assembly member, Dakshayani Velayudhan, like Ambedkar, was born in a Dalit family and consequently, struggled to get an education. She was the only Dalit woman member of the Constituent Assembly and stood up in support of Ambedkar on reservation for Dalits. Their words carried weight because they were two members who had personal knowledge of what a Dalit faced from Hindu society and were ready to fight for their rights.

Most of the women had illustrious careers after their stint in the Assembly. Many became members of Parliament, got involved in social work, became ministers and were honoured by national awards. Sucheta Kripalani became India's first woman Chief Minister when she led the government of Uttar Pradesh. Sarojini Naidu had become Governor of the state earlier. Malati Choudhury was a member of the Planning Commission and in 1975, during the Emergency declared by Prime Minister Indira Gandhi, she led protests that resulted in imprisonment. Rajkumari Amrit Kaur, appointed Minister of Health in Nehru's first cabinet, came from the royal family of Kapurthala. She was the founder of the All India Institute of Medical Sciences (AIIMS) and the Tuberculosis Association of India. Vijaya Lakshmi Pandit became a diplomat and was the first woman and the first Asian to be appointed as the President of the United Nations General Assembly.

A Forgotten Voice

The life of Jaipal Singh was as remarkable as that of Ambedkar. He was born in the Munda tribe of Chota Nagpur in south Bihar and spoke up for the rights of the tribal people in the Assembly. He was born in a poor family and sent off to herd sheep, but his intelligence was noticed by missionaries who sent him to school and then to a college in Ranchi. Through hard work and sheer brilliance, Jaipal Singh got to St John's College in Oxford, earning an honours degree in Economics. A brilliant sportsman, he was the captain of the Indian hockey team that won the gold medal at the Olympics in 1928.

Jaipal Singh made the Assembly conscious of the condition of tribals who he called 'Adibasi' or the original inhabitants of India and fought for the need for them to get the same reservations as Dalits. A brilliant orator, he began his first speech, 'As a junglee, as an adibasi . . .' and went on to say, 'The whole history of my people is one of continuous exploitation and dispossession.' In 1938, he had founded the Adibasi Sabha and demanded a separate state for tribals called Jharkhand. Today, we do have a state but in many ways the social and economic condition of the adivasis still remains backward as their rights to their land and their way of life are still in danger while modern facilities of education and health care are not provided by the government.

The Backroom Boys

The Constituent Assembly was a microcosm of India and was a perfect reflection of its many opinions, expectations and suggestions. Members were suggesting and debating many clauses. At the same time, there were appeals and recommendations pouring in from every corner of the country. Debates would get heated as every member had their own ideas; so the seven-member Drafting Committee had a tough job to do and it needed a full team of bureaucrats to help them. So the Committee was assisted by the Constituent Assembly Secretariat that first drafted the Constitution and then later, helped prepare the first electoral rolls for elections. The first elections were held between 25 October 1951 to 21 February 1952 and we had 17.3 crore voters.

One can easily imagine the challenge Ambedkar and the Drafting Committee faced as every idea approved by the Assembly finally landed on their desk. As they worked on the contents of the constitution, they were framing the birth of a nation and every sentence and word had to be chosen with great thought; every comma and full stop placed with care. After all, this was a document whose clauses could affect the lives of people and could also be questioned in a court of law.

I HAVE AN IDEA!

SUBMISSIONS TO THE CONSTITUENT ASSEMBLY CAME POURING IN FROM ALL ACROSS THE COUNTRY, INCLUDING SUCH DIVERSE ORGANIZATIONS AS THE CALCUTTA BAR ASSOCIATION; THE DISTRICT TEACHER'S GUILD OF VIZIANAGARAM AND THE CENTRAL JEWISH BOARD OF BOMBAY. EVERYONE HAD AN IDEA AND THEY ALL WANTED TO BE HEARD.

In this job, Ambedkar was helped by two men who are rarely credited for their extraordinary contributions and relentless hard work. There was B.N. Rau, the Constitutional Adviser who was a leading jurist and would one day represent India in the United Nation Security Council. A former member of the Indian Civil Service, he had travelled widely across the world, visiting democracies like the USA, UK, Canada and Ireland, met legal and constitution experts and spoke to many judges. Rau studied all the important constitutions of the world and his opinion on every clause was heard in the Assembly's inner councils.

Then there was the Chief Drafting Officer S.N. Mukherjee, joint secretary in the Secretariat who wrote the first draft of the actual text that was then discussed by the committee and then presented to the Assembly. According to Ambedkar, Mukherjee's 'ability to put the most intricate proposals in the simplest and clearest legal form can rarely be equalled . . .' Whenever Rau drafted any clause, he would pass it to Mukherjee who would write it in the correct legal language.

THE CORE TEAM

THE TEAM AT THE SECRETARIAT COMPRISED OF S.N. MUKHERJEE, DEPUTY SECRETARY & CHIEF DRAFTSMAN; K.V. PADMANABHAN, UNDER SECRETARY; P.S. SUBRAMANIAN, UNDER SECRETARY; A.A. ABIDI, RESEARCH OFFICER AND BRIJ BHUSHAN, RESEARCH OFFICER.

It was the members of the Constituent Assembly Secretariat who handled the hundreds of queries and suggestions pouring in from all across India and through their correspondence, they gained an invaluable knowledge of the country. Among the committee members, Ambedkar depended most on Alladi Krishnaswamy Ayyar, who was a former Advocate General of Madras State. Always generous with his praise, Ambedkar said, 'There were in the drafting committee men bigger, better and more competent than myself such as my friend Sir Alladi Krishnaswamy Ayyar.'

SUCH A BIG DOCUMENT

S.N. MUKHERJEE EXPLAINED WHY THE
CONSTITUTION OF INDIA WAS SO BIG. A VERY
PRACTICAL MAN, HE WAS SAYING THAT AS
INDIA WAS SUCH A HUGE AND COMPLICATED
COUNTRY FULL OF PEOPLE ALWAYS READY
TO QUESTION AND DEBATE, IT WAS BETTER
TO SPELL EVERYTHING OUT IN DETAIL SO
THAT THERE IS MINIMUM CONFUSION OR
COMPLICATIONS.

The leaders could give impassioned speeches on the floor of the Assembly. There could be long debates in private gatherings but when it came to the actual work of drafting the words, Rau and Mukherjee were trusted to do the job. They were experts at drafting legal documents and ensuring that it reflected the opinion of the Assembly. They knew that leaving loopholes could lead the document to be exploited later. Energy, meticulous attention to detail; knowledge of constitutional law and intense hard work were the characteristics of these backroom boys of the Constituent Assembly Secretariat, who worked quietly behind the scenes. Ambedkar gave much of the credit for the success of his project to Rau, Mukherjee and Ayyar. So we'll end with the words of Ayyar, who supported universal adult franchise and said, 'Citizenship carried with it rights as well as obligations.'

CHAPTER FIVE

FOR THE PEOPLE
FUNDAMENTAL RIGHTS AND DIRECTIVE PRINCIPLES

'If we wish to maintain democracy not merely in form; but also in fact, what must we do? The first thing in my judgement we must do is to hold fast to constitutional methods of achieving our social and economic objectives.'

B.R. AMBEDKAR

The Constitution of India was not just about laws and the government, it also aimed to start a social revolution in a country that was very poor, divided and unequal. As a matter of fact, many in the West thought that in a country where a majority of the population was illiterate, we were being very ambitious talking of fundamental rights— but what they did not appreciate was that our freedom fighters had been talking about it throughout over six decades of our freedom struggle and there was quite a lot of awareness among the people.

At the core of this social revolution were the sections on Fundamental Rights and Directive Principles that began by declaring that all Indians were equal before the law. It did not matter if we were rich or poor, a man, woman or child, a Hindu, Muslim or Sikh, from a caste considered high or low, living in Tamil Nadu, Assam or Kashmir, vegetarian or otherwise. We were all proudly Indian and we were just as proudly equal.

The Fundamental Rights and the Directive Principles were spelled out in Part III and IV of the Constitution and these are not dry-as-dust laws or complicated ideas. They are rights that affect the lives of every Indian citizen. We all understand equality and freedom, don't we? They are our fundamental rights. During the time when the British ruled India, these rights that we call 'fundamental' were not given to Indians. For example, the police could arrest anyone without a warrant and keep them in jail without a trial. There was no equality and only a few chosen people were allowed to vote. So even today, it is important for us to be aware of our fundamental rights.

THE CONSCIENCE OF THE CONSTITUTION

THIS IS WHAT HISTORIAN GRANVILLE AUSTIN SAYS ABOUT THE SECTION ON FUNDAMENTAL RIGHTS, 'THE INDIAN CONSTITUTION IS FIRST AND FOREMOST A SOCIAL DOCUMENT . . . THE CORE OF THE COMMITMENT TO THE SOCIAL REVOLUTION LIES IN PART III AND IV, IN THE FUNDAMENTAL RIGHTS AND IN THE DIRECTIVE PRINCIPLES OF STATE POLICY. THESE ARE THE CONSCIENCE OF THE CONSTITUTION.'

AS AUSTIN SAYS, THIS CONSTITUTION IS THINKING OF THE PEOPLE FIRST AND ACTS AS THE CONSCIENCE OF OUR LEADERS, MAKING SURE THAT THEY GIVE PRIORITY TO THE BENEFITS OF THE PEOPLE. LATER HE WRITES, 'THEY WERE INCLUDED IN THE CONSTITUTION IN THE HOPE AND EXPECTATION THAT ONE DAY THE TREE OF TRUE LIBERTY WOULD BLOOM IN INDIA.'

How do the Fundamental Rights affect the lives of common people? They give us the right to live anywhere we want, do any work we desire, follow any religion we like or even choose not to follow any religion at all. For example, you can be a lover of nature and start a new religion that worships trees or birds and the Constitution says you have the right to do so.

No one can declare, 'You are a Dalit or a girl and therefore, you can't do this.' So if a Dalit is not allowed into a hotel or is refused a job on the basis of his/her caste, he/she has the right to go to court. Just as in 2018, the Supreme Court declared that women cannot be stopped from praying at the Sabarimala temple, where previously, women under the age of fifty were not permitted to enter. People may weep and wail about their religious rights, they may claim they are talking directly to the gods but equality always comes first. It says so in the Preamble.

We have freedom of speech and that includes a free press; all of us have the right to express our opinion in newspapers, books, and on television and now on new platforms like social media. The atrocious horror of the caste system has been made illegal and we are all equal before the law. So citizens are protected not only from a dictatorial government but also from exploitation by the rich and powerful and the evils of inhumane social traditions. If our rights are threatened, we can first appeal to the police and then to the judiciary to protect us. As we have seen in the years since the Constitution was adopted, the Supreme Court has often stepped forward to protect our fundamental rights.

The Fundamental Rights are at the heart of our democracy because they give us the right to live in freedom as equal citizens. During the years of the freedom struggle, the British government had declared that one of the reasons that they were still ruling India was to protect the rights of the religious minorities like the Muslims and Christians against the danger they would face from a Hindu majority. So the members of the Constituent Assembly took great pains to ensure that all Indians were treated as equals before the law and that they all had the same rights and freedoms.

> ## VOICES
>
> SARDAR PATEL WAS VERY KEEN TO ENSURE THAT THE RIGHTS OF ALL MINORITIES BE PROTECTED AND DECLARED, 'IT IS FOR US TO PROVE . . . NOBODY CAN BE MORE INTERESTED THAN US IN INDIA, IN THE PROTECTION OF OUR MINORITIES. OUR MISSION IS TO SATISFY EVERY ONE OF THEM . . .'

The Directive Principles are more like instructions from the Constitution to the government and sets down guidelines for the legislatures and executives of both the Indian States and the Central government. Like the Fundamental Rights, it instructs the government on the duties of the State towards its citizens. It tells them what to do for the benefit of the citizens. The Principles range from the rights of workers to equal pay for men and women; health care for all and the organization of village panchayats. The Directive Principles spell out how the promises made in the Preamble are to be carried out by the government.

RAISING THEIR VOICE

THE SUBCOMMITTEE THAT WAS RESPONSIBLE FOR DRAFTING THE FUNDAMENTAL RIGHTS INCLUDED TWO WOMEN—RAJKUMARI AMRIT KAUR AND HANSA MEHTA. AT A TIME WHEN MANY MEN FELT WOMEN DID NOT DESERVE EQUAL RIGHTS, THEY SPOKE UP FOR THE RIGHTS OF WOMEN.

AMONG THE PROPOSALS PUT BEFORE THE COMMITTEE WAS A VERY DANGEROUS IDEA—THE RIGHT TO BEAR ARMS, LIKE IN THE UNITED STATES. FORTUNATELY, IT WAS PROMPTLY REJECTED BY A COMMITTEE THAT BELIEVED IN AHIMSA.

The people drafting the Fundamental Rights had to think hard about what they were doing and the effect it would have on society. Not everyone wanted equality and freedom for all Indians. For example, there were many conservative and superstitious people who opposed a law that banned untouchability because they belonged to the upper castes and had much to gain from perpetuating the caste system. Similarly, there were men who felt that women should not be given the right to vote. And sadly, all these years later, there are people among us who still believe that. Luckily, the Constitution stands by us when our rights are challenged by narrow-minded people. The committee drafting the Fundamental Rights knew that there would always be people who would try to take advantage of the rights offered to them, especially when the government tried to introduce social reform, which is why they framed the rights very carefully.

For example, in the beginning, there was a right to property and that clashed with the government's efforts at land reform. At that time, most of the land was owned by big landowners called zamindars, who led luxurious lives in the cities while the farmers who did all the work were paid a pittance. This was one of the causes of poverty in rural areas. The government decided to give the land to the farmers and zamindari was banned. The landowners immediately proclaimed that their fundamental rights of property were being attacked and went to court. The Parliament then had to pass an amendment to make the land reforms work.

Similarly, the right to religion worried many women like Rajkumari Amrit Kaur because men could try to bring back evil practices like sati or even untouchability by claiming that it was part of their religion. So sati had been legally banned in the nineteenth century during the British period and the practice had died out; untouchability was now banned in the Constitution. It was made clear that our right to life, liberty and equality comes first.

The Fundamental Rights were finalized after years of hard work. Many people wrote in their suggestions and at times, questionnaires were sent out to understand people's views and opinions. There were long discussions and often, pretty heated arguments in the Constituent Assembly, until the final structure took shape at last.

Fundamental Rights

The framing of the Fundamental Rights was influenced by the Bill of Rights of the United States of America and the Declaration of Human Rights of the United Nations but the roots lay in the six decades of our freedom struggle. During that time, the freedom fighters, especially of the Congress Party, became conscious of what these rights had to be so that they could begin a social revolution in India. They understood very well that when people were assured of freedom, equality and religious tolerance in the Constitution, they would gain the courage to work for their future.

Unlike the constitution of Great Britain, we chose to write down the Fundamental Rights. This was for two reasons. First, as a former colony, we had a healthy suspicion of the government's ability to protect us. Second, as Sardar Patel said, we needed to allay any fear that the minority communities had about their rights being overwhelmed by the majority (Hindus made up over 80 per cent of the population).

The Fundamental Rights are stated in Part III of the Constitution and the six Fundamental Rights that are recognized by the Constitution are:

- Right to Equality
- Right to Freedom
- Right Against Exploitation
- Right to Freedom of Religion
- Cultural and Educational Rights
- The Right to Constitutional Remedies

So this is a charter of rights that guarantees basic civil liberties like equality and freedom that our freedom fighters had to fight for and that we take for granted today. The makers of our constitution hoped that by stating the Fundamental Rights clearly in writing, we will be able give the people the opportunity to live in peace and harmony. For the first time in centuries, the poor of the country—especially the Dalits—were given simple human dignity and the right to dream of a better life. The upper castes of Hindu society were not interested in fighting the evils of the caste system, so Ambedkar and his enlightened team began the battle. And even today, the struggle goes on.

WE EAT TOGETHER

WHEN GANDHIJI FIRST ATTENDED THE SESSIONS OF THE CONGRESS PARTY, HE DISCOVERED THAT UPPER CASTE MEMBERS LIVED AND ATE SEPARATELY. AS THE LEADER, HE MADE SURE THAT EVERYONE LIVED TOGETHER AND ATE TOGETHER. HE EVEN MADE THEM USE BROOMS TO CLEAN THE VENUE!

Fundamental rights are basic human freedoms that every democracy in the world guarantees and it has a long history. When the British government introduced their system of education in India, our students learnt about England's Bill of Rights (1689); The Bill of Rights in the Constitution of the United States of America (1791) and France's Declaration of the Rights of Man (1789). Finally, there was the Universal Declaration of Human Rights that was adopted by the United Nations General Assembly in 1948. So an education in English made young Indians conscious of their rights!

In our constitution were added the rights needed to fight the many social evils that were unique to India, such as the caste system that allowed untouchability, people being discriminated against because of their religion and a person's ethnic background according to the region of birth or their gender. That meant no one could be treated as unequal if you were a Dalit, a woman or belonged to any region. Most importantly, the Fundamental Rights protect the citizen from both the action of the government and also of other people. However, the freedoms guaranteed by the Fundamental Rights are not absolute, they are not written in stone. They can be changed by a constitutional amendment and they can be put on hold if an Emergency is declared, as it happened in 1975.

The Constitution gave us the rights but it did not mean people would automatically obey the laws. For example, a big landowner who enslaved Dalits and forced them to do free labour in a system called *begar* would just ignore their right to freedom and fair pay. Businessmen may refuse to offer jobs to candidates on the basis of their religion or gender. So the Constitution gave people the option to go to the law courts to seek help in protecting their rights. If anyone feels that their Fundamental Rights are being threatened, they can appeal directly to the Supreme Court.

AMENDMENTS

THE CONSTITUENT ASSEMBLY MADE IT VERY DIFFICULT TO CHANGE A FUNDAMENTAL RIGHT. IT REQUIRES A CONSTITUTIONAL AMENDMENT THAT HAS TO BE PASSED BY BOTH HOUSES OF THE PARLIAMENT BY A SPECIAL MAJORITY. USUALLY, ACTS ARE PASSED BY A SIMPLE MAJORITY, THAT IS, MORE THAN HALF THE VOTES CAST. HOWEVER, FOR A CONSTITUTIONAL AMENDMENT TO BE PASSED, YOU NEED TWO-THIRDS OF THE VOTES IN BOTH THE LOK SABHA AND THE RAJYA SABHA.

Right to Equality

The Right to Equality is the first and most important of the Fundamental Rights and all the other rights and liberties flow from it. We are all equal before the law—not just adults but even children. No government or court of law can say that a rich person has more rights than a poor one; neither can they say that a man's evidence will be given more weight than that of a woman, as some religious laws do.

Equality also meant that no one could be stopped from using any public places and amenities such as parks, railway stations, temples, ponds and wells. Ambedkar understood this very well as he had led a protest at a tank where Dalits were not allowed to use water and fought for their right to enter temples. This kind of discrimination was not unique to India. For example, the blacks in

South Africa and the United States were prevented from entering restaurants, sit in the front seats of a bus or even drink from the same water fountain that everyone else used. This also meant that no one can be stopped from entering a place of worship or be stopped from living anywhere.

A serious effort was made to help the poor and the Dalits. By Article 17, untouchability was abolished and this meant that if anyone practiced untouchability, they could be sent to jail. Forced labour or begar was banned. The Right to Equality meant that everyone can study in any school or college and apply for a government job.

SIR, I AM NOT REFUSING YOU A JOB ON THE BASIS OF YOUR RELIGION, BUT YOUR QUALIFICATION IS M.A. HISTORY, WHATSAPP UNIVERSITY!?

Here, our constitution moved to help the weaker sections of society like the Dalits and tribals who were poor and had faced discrimination from society for centuries. They faced huge challenges in getting education or jobs and without the support of the government, they could not get them. So the people belonging to the Scheduled Castes and Scheduled Tribes were given reservations in educational institutions like schools and colleges and then in government jobs too.

Right to Freedom

You may think, so what's so special about freedom? We are all free, aren't we? Today, we take freedom for granted. You must not forget that during the years when India was a British colony, Indians were not free. The Constitution guarantees the right to life and personal liberty. There are many facets to freedom and the right to freedom can be divided into six sections. However, it is important to know that all of them are on condition that they are not against the law, against public order or against the sovereignty and integrity of India. We are not allowed to take advantage of this Fundamental Right for our selfish reasons.

Freedom of speech and expression includes, most importantly, the freedom of the press. Try to imagine a future in which you can't get the news through newspapers, television and social media because there is censorship imposed by the government. The people in power could then do anything they wanted to, and we would not even know about it. Of course, this does not mean we can write anything we want, if it is wrong or is against the public good. One of the best examples of a threat to this right is fake news on social media. In many ways, the trolls on social media are acting against freedom of speech as they are abusing someone and that is against the law. You can complain against trolls to the police and take them to court.

Freedom to assemble peaceably and without arms means we can assemble to protest but the campaign has to be peaceful. We don't have the right to carry arms or become violent, so waving about sticks, guns or even *trishul*s is against the law. The government has the right to check or even ban protests for the safety of citizens and to maintain public order.

Freedom to form associations and unions is the right to form organizations like trade unions that protect the rights of workers.

Freedom to move freely throughout the territory of India means we have the right to travel anywhere in the country unless there are restrictions placed on certain regions, for example, during epidemics or riots.

Freedom to reside and settle in any part of the territory of India means we can live and work anywhere in India but again, the government has the right to place reasonable restrictions like preventing people from moving into tribal areas or to protect the environment.

Freedom to practice any profession means we can do any work we want as long as it does not endanger people or is illegal, like selling drugs.

A FUNDAMENTAL RIGHT FOR CHILDREN

IN 2002, BY THE EIGHTY-SIXTH AMENDMENT TO THE CONSTITUTION, ALL CHILDREN WERE GIVEN THE RIGHT TO PRIMARY EDUCATION. IT STATES THAT THE STATE HAS TO PROVIDE FREE AND COMPULSORY EDUCATION TO CHILDREN FROM THE AGE OF SIX TO FOURTEEN.

Right Against Exploitation

It is a sad fact of our world that powerful people exploit the weak and as the landowners supported the British they were allowed to get away with practices that were against basic human rights. As mentioned earlier, due to the long-established system of begar rich landowners would make the farm labourers work for free; they would give them nothing besides food. Poor people, who often could not read or write, would sometimes take a loan and go on doing begar for decades, thinking that they still hadn't paid off the loan. This right also bans children below the age of fourteen to be employed in dangerous jobs.

SPEAKING UP IN PROTEST

MANY WRITERS, LIKE PREMCHAND, WROTE PIECES IN PROTEST OF THE EXPLOITATION OF FARMERS. THERE WERE FILMS LIKE *DO BIGHA ZAMEEN* THAT SHOWED US HOW AN HONEST FARMER LOST HIS LAND TO CROOKED ZAMINDARS. *NIL DARPAN* BY DINABANDHU MITRA, PUBLISHED IN 1860, IS ABOUT THE EXPLOITATION OF FARMERS BY OWNERS OF INDIGO PLANTATIONS.

Right to Freedom of Religion

We have the right to follow any religion we want and even have the right to not follow any religion at all. This is where the concept of secularism comes in. In the West, secularism means religion is considered a personal matter and the State completely denies the role of religion in public life. In India, we interpret secularism a bit differently. The Constitution recognizes the presence of religion in our lives. Before the government and the law, all religions are equal and no religion can be favoured over another. Just because you belong to the majority religion does not mean you can take the law into your own hands.

Citizens are free to practise whatever religion they want, they can preach and spread their faith. We have the right to change our religion too. We respect all religions—that means Hindus can light up their homes on Diwali, a Christian can sing carols for Christmas and a Muslim can celebrate Id by eating the traditional biryani—and in an ideal world, we can all celebrate these religious festivals together.

Indians are a very religious people and four of the world religions have begun in India—Hinduism, Buddhism, Jainism and Sikhism. Secularism is crucial in a country that has people following at least seven religions and an endless variation of faiths. Without tolerance of the practices of other religions, India can lose its fragile unity. Great kings in the past, from Ashoka to Krishnadevaraya and Akbar, recognized this and they welcomed all religions. Ashoka never insisted that people convert to Buddhism. Krishnadevaraya had Muslim generals in his army who took their oath of loyalty on the Quran. Many of the Mughal kings were surprisingly secular and it began with Akbar, who married Hindu princesses and happily joined them in playing Holi. His grandson Shahjahan's grandmother and mother were Rajput princesses and so he was three quarters Hindu. Secular Indians understand that all religions are really just saying the same things—be truthful, kind, compassionate, generous and tolerant.

VOICES

'WE HAVE LAID DOWN IN OUR CONSTITUTION THAT INDIA IS A SECULAR STATE. THAT DOES NOT MEAN IRRELIGION. IT MEANS EQUAL RESPECT FOR ALL FAITHS AND EQUAL OPPORTUNITIES FOR THOSE WHO PROFESS ANY FAITH.'—JAWAHARLAL NEHRU

Cultural and Educational Rights

India is a very complex country—there are so many languages, religions and cultures that sometimes it seems very hard to reach out to everyone. There are twenty-two national languages and any community that has a language and a script of its own has the right to protect and develop it. For most people, their culture—language and literature, music, dance, painting and sculpture—is a part of their roots and the Constitution respects that. No one can be discriminated against when getting education or a job or any government benefit on the basis of their language and culture. This means you cannot be refused a job or a seat in a college just because you don't speak Hindi. This also means you can establish educational institutions to develop your culture; however, when it comes to the important matter of education, the State has the right to supervise what is being taught in schools run by minorities and religious organizations.

Right to Constitutional Remedies

What does 'constitutional remedies' mean? It means that any citizen who feels his or her fundamental right has been denied can go to the law courts and demand a trial. For example, if someone has been arrested, the police has to tell the court the reason for the arrest and the citizen has the right to get a lawyer and fight the case. The police has to produce the arrested person in court by a writ called *habeas corpus*. This right is suspended when an Emergency is declared.

RIGHT TO PROPERTY

THIS HAS BEEN A CONTROVERSIAL FUNDAMENTAL RIGHT AND AFTER AMENDMENTS, IS NOW JUST A RIGHT. ORIGINALLY, THE CONSTITUTION GAVE ALL CITIZENS THE RIGHT TO BUY AND SELL PROPERTY AND ARTICLE 31 SAID THAT 'NO PERSON SHALL BE DEPRIVED OF HIS PROPERTY SAVE BY AUTHORITY OF THE LAW'. ALSO, IF ANYONE'S PROPERTY WAS TAKEN OVER BY THE GOVERNMENT, THE OWNER HAD TO BE PAID COMPENSATION.

THEN AMENDMENTS HAD TO BE PASSED TO
ALLOW FOR LAND REFORMS, LIKE BANNING
THE ZAMINDARI SYSTEM. THE CONTROVERSIES
GO ON TO THIS DAY. THERE HAVE BEEN
CASES WHERE LAND HAS BEEN TAKEN BY
THE GOVERNMENT FOR PURPOSES LIKE
BUILDING ROADS OR ECONOMIC ZONES AND
THE FARMERS HAVE PROTESTED. THIS RIGHT
HAS BEEN AMENDED MANY TIMES OVER
THE YEARS AND REMAINS A MATTER THAT
EVEN THE GOVERNMENT AND THE JUDICIARY
DO NOT AGREE UPON.

If you think about it, the Fundamental Rights encompass within them the dream of a newly independent nation. It says, *this is what we Indians want to be—free, equal and secular.* These men and women working for years to carefully draft each word were following what Mahatma Gandhi had been talking about throughout the freedom movement. We had to take our future in our hands and build a nation that we could be proud of. Next to the Preamble, the Fundamental Rights are at the heart of our Constitution.

Directive Principles

The Directive Principles of State Policy is like the citizens of the country telling the government what it should do. It instructs the Central and State governments on its duties towards its citizens. However, there is an important difference between the section on Fundamental Rights and Directive Principles. The latter cannot be challenged in a court of law and that means that we cannot appeal to the judiciary to make the government follow any Directive Principle. These are guidelines to the Central and State governments that they should keep in mind while they make laws or plan any policy. It aims to create social and economic conditions under which Indian citizens can lead a good life and that includes the rights of children.

If you look at them carefully, you will realize that the Fundamental Rights protect our civil and political rights like freedom and equality and the Directive Principles talk of our social and economic welfare like health services and livelihood. So it is stating the aims of the government and instructing it on its duties. It is, in some ways, reaching for an ideal, and in the last seventy years, we have achieved some and failed to achieve many of its aims. For example, we still have a serious inequality in incomes and children are still being exploited and made to work when they should be at school.

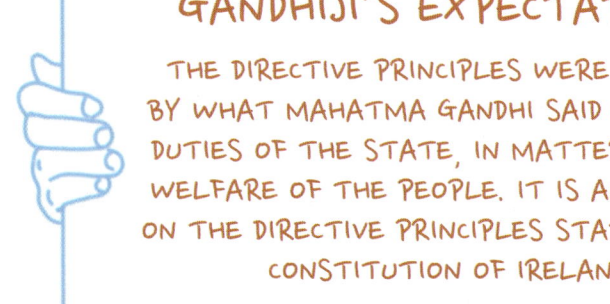

GANDHIJI'S EXPECTATIONS

THE DIRECTIVE PRINCIPLES WERE INSPIRED BY WHAT MAHATMA GANDHI SAID WERE THE DUTIES OF THE STATE, IN MATTERS OF THE WELFARE OF THE PEOPLE. IT IS ALSO BASED ON THE DIRECTIVE PRINCIPLES STATED IN THE CONSTITUTION OF IRELAND.

The Directive Principles say that the State has to provide adequate means of livelihood for people, with equal pay for men and women. It has to make sure that all the wealth is not concentrated in the hands of a few people, leading to economic inequality. It talks of the right to work and the right to humane conditions at work. Workers should receive a fair wage and the State should establish a minimum pay. It is also the State's responsibility to help the weaker sections of society in improving their lives.

The Directive Principles cover a wide variety of subjects like providing health care and improving agriculture; protecting the environment and wildlife and the preservation of historical monuments. The government has to organize village panchayats and encourage them to improve the economic conditions of villages.

RIGHTS VS DIRECTIVES

LAWS HAVE A WAY OF GETTING COMPLICATED. SO IF THERE IS A CONFLICT BETWEEN A FUNDAMENTAL RIGHT AND A DIRECTIVE PRINCIPLE AND THE PEOPLE APPEAL TO THE COURTS, THEN THE DIRECTIVE PRINCIPLE GETS PRIORITY (IF IT IS FOR THE COMMON GOOD). THE BEST EXAMPLE IS LAND REFORM, WHERE LAND HELD BY ZAMINDARS WAS DISTRIBUTED TO THE DALIT AND LANDLESS POOR AND THE FUNDAMENTAL RIGHT TO PROPERTY WAS AMENDED BY THE PARLIAMENT.

The Directive Principles expect the government in the Centre and the States to ensure the following things:

- Promote a social order in which there is social, economic and political justice in all institutions of life.
- The State will work to reduce inequality in the economic state of people and also in opportunities and social status.
- The State has to try to provide an adequate means of livelihood for all its citizens, both men and women. It also has to guarantee equal pay for equal work for men and women.
- The State should prevent wealth and the means being concentrated in the control of a few people.
- Workers and children should not be exploited, not just by the government but also by the industry and even in private homes.
- Provide free legal aid for those who are too poor to pay for it.
- Organize village panchayats and ensure they are run in a fair and equal manner.
- Help people who are unemployed, old or disabled to get work.
- Workers should get a fair living wage, have good working conditions and get the opportunity for paid leave.
- Promote cottage industries.
- Raise the level of nutrition and standard of living.
- Improve public health.

- Promote scientific agriculture.
- Protect the environment, forest and wildlife of the country.
- Protect monuments and all places of historic and artistic importance.
- Separate the judiciary and the executive in public service.

Looking back to the last several decades, we realize that there is much that is still left to be achieved but there has been quite a lot of work done to improve the life of the people. Among the achievements have been a number of Land Reform Acts that have given the right of ownership of the land to the farmers who cultivate it. Till 2001, over two crore acres or eighty thousand kilometres of land has been handed over to the landless poor. Then there is the Consumer Protection Act of 1986 that offers protection to consumers. The Equal Remuneration Act of 1976 promises equal pay for equal work for men and women. The Sampoorna Grameen Rozgar Yojana of 2001 promises employment to the poor in rural areas. The establishment of the system of Panchayati Raj in villages now has one-third of the seats in panchayats being reserved for women. The Central government has launched a number of national programmes that aim at the welfare of the people. Among them are the National Rural Employment Programme (MNREGA), the National Rural Health Mission and recently the Swachh Bharat programme. These have made a big difference in the life of people in villages.

Fundamental Duties

If the Constitution was talking of our rights and the duties of the government, it also tells us the duties of the citizens of India. After all, if the Constitution gives us so much, it also has the right to expect something from us.

Here are the Fundamental Duties:

- Abide by the Constitution and respect the ideals and institutions, the national flag and the national anthem.
- Cherish and follow the noble ideals which inspired India's struggle for freedom.
- Uphold and protest the sovereignty, unity and integrity of India.
- Defend the country and render national service when called upon to do so.
- Promote harmony and the spirit of brotherhood beyond religious, linguistic, regional and sectional diversities; renounce practices derogatory to women.
- Value and preserve the rich heritage of our composite culture.
- Protect and improve the environment.
- Develop a scientific temper, humanism and the spirit of inquiry and reform.
- Safeguard public property and abjure violence.
- Strive towards excellence in all sphere of individual and collective activity so that the nation constantly rises to higher levels of endeavour and achievement.
- Provide opportunities for education to one's child between the ages of six and fourteen.

So far, we have been judging the record of the government in matters of Fundamental Rights and Directive Principles and many times, found it wanting. If we now look at ourselves and what we have done about the duties of a citizen, the picture is not too encouraging, is it? Indians are still twisted into the coils of the caste system—Dalits, the poor and women in our society often face social prejudice and get lower wages. We are still making children work when they should be in school. Many of us are extremely intolerant of other religions, especially of Islam, and minority communities face both social rejection and violence, using religion as an excuse. Even people who come from other regions and therefore speak a different language face our prejudice. Indians often talk about how tolerant and humane we are, but are we sure that we are?

Some of us prefer mythology to scientific facts and reject logic and choose superstition. We get angry very easily and at every riot, the first thing we turn our rage to is public property, such as buses and trains. We do not respect the environment and are constantly trying to encroach forest lands that belong to tribal people. Meanwhile, the rich avoid paying taxes and park their money abroad. This is the sad reality of our country today.

Looking at the clauses of the Fundamental Rights, Directive Principles and Fundamental Duties, do you think the citizens of India are good, law-abiding citizens?

CHAPTER SIX

HOW DOES OUR GOVERNMENT WORK?

The future evolution of the Indian Constitution will
thus depend to a large extent upon the Supreme Court
and the direction given to it by that Court . . . It is
the great tribunal which has to draw the line between
liberty and social control.'

ALLADI KRISHNASWAMI AYYAR

The Constitution of India is not just about our rights, it is also about a very practical and very important matter—how is the government to be run? It is fine to talk about equality and freedom but there is the matter of running schools and hospitals; electricity supply and garbage collection; roads to be built and train stations to be run; taxes to be collected and criminals to be caught and punished. A government is a giant and very complex enterprise and we had to lay down the rules for it.

Imagine the architects of our Constitution sitting there and creating a structure of government while trying to anticipate the problems that such a government could face sometime in the far future. Just to give you an example, in 1947, there were no cyber-crimes or fake news; our politicians did not have criminal backgrounds and there were no suicide bombers. It is remarkable how well the Constitution has managed to evolve to meet every challenge so far.

Our leaders looked around and there were many kinds of government in the world. There was the presidential system of the United States of America; the elected executive system of Switzerland and then there was the parliamentary system of Great Britain that was headed by a prime minister. We chose the British system with an elected Parliament that elected a prime minister who appoints his cabinet. However, there was one difference between India and Britain. The head of the executive branch in Britain is the monarch, we have an elected President. Our government is divided into three branches—the Executive, the Legislature and the Judiciary. In matters of power, they are placed in positions of equality, thus acting as checks and balances to ensure that no one branch could dominate or control the government. The actual work of running the country is done by the bureaucracy in various ministries headed by civil servants.

The country was divided into states and each state had its own government in what is called a federal system. This could lead to conflict between the Central and State governments about their roles. So the Constitution has three lists—The Union List, about matters that can only be acted upon by the central Parliament; the State List, i.e., the area of the state legislatures and the Concurrent List, which is under the power of both—but if there is any conflict, then the Union's law is given preference. So matters of national importance (such as defence, elections or foreign affairs) are in the Union List; law and order, prisons and inmates, agriculture or water supply are in the State List but there is a lot of overlap in the Concurrent List.

Basic Structure

One of the earliest challenges to the constitution was around the land reforms being carried out by the government. In 1950 much of the land was owned by the zamindars and religious organizations like temples and ashrams. The farmers who did the work of cultivation had to give away a large part of their crops as rent. The government decided to change this and set a limit to how much land anyone could own. The rest of the land was given to the farmers. This naturally made the landowners very angry and they challenged the reforms in the Supreme Court saying that this affected their right to property.

This question was answered by the Kesavananda Bharati case. The Supreme Court declared in the Kesavananda Bharati case in 1973 that the Constitution has a 'basic structure' that cannot be changed. Kesavananda, as the head of a religious organization that owned a lot of land, had challenged the Kerala government's efforts at land reform by giving land to the farmers. The Supreme Court declared that right to property could not be a fundamental right because social justice was more important. The Constitution makes it clear that the welfare of the poor will always come first.

As Justice S.M. Sikri explained, the basic structure includes among others the supremacy of the Constitution; its secular character; that power is to be divided between the executive, legislature and judiciary branches of the government; free and fair elections; fundamental rights, directive principles, and freedom and equality of all citizens. This means that if any amendment of the Constitution is passed by Parliament that the Supreme Court feels would alter this basic structure, it can cancel it. So a political party with a majority in Parliament that thinks it can change the Constitution through amendments can be challenged in the Supreme Court and it can be struck down if the Court feels it is against the basic structure of the Constitution.

The Executive: The President, the Prime Minister, the Council of Ministers

India's parliamentary system is very similar to the British system except for one crucial difference. We do not have a hereditary monarch. Instead, we have an elected President as the symbolic head of the State. Unlike the members of Parliament and legislative assemblies, the citizens do not vote for the President. He is elected by what is called an Electoral College that includes the members of the Lok Sabha and Rajya Sabha, or the MPs; and the members of the Legislative Assemblies of the States and the Union Territories or the MLAs. He is elected for a term of five years and he can be re-elected for a second term. Till date, India's first President, Rajendra Prasad is the only President to have served two terms.

Now what does a President do and what is his role as the head of the executive branch of the government? First, after elections, he appoints the prime minister and his ministers and gives the oath of office. He also appoints the chief justice of the Supreme Court, the Governors of the states and officials like the election commissioner, the comptroller, auditor general, and the attorney general. However, the President does not make these appointments independently, he only makes them on the advice of the prime minister. The President is the Head of State but he does not run the country.

According to the Constitution, the President acts on the advice of the prime minister and his cabinet but the President is not a mere figurehead and has an active role to play in executive and legislative matters. For example, when an election produces a fractured result with no political party getting a clear majority, his role becomes very important because we cannot let the engine of government stop at any time. It is the President who decides which party is to be invited to form the government and then that political party has to prove its majority in the Lok Sabha. He can dissolve the Lok Sabha if the party in power loses its majority and call for fresh elections.

The President is the supreme commander of the armed forces and that is why he takes the salute at the parade on Republic Day. He has the power of pardon as the final appeal for people who have been given the death sentence by law courts. He can grant a pardon or change the sentence to imprisonment.

PRESIDENTIAL HOMES

WE ARE ALL FAMILIAR WITH THE MAJESTIC RASHTRAPATI BHAVAN, THE PRESIDENT'S HOME IN DELHI. HE ALSO HAS TWO MORE RESIDENCES— THE RETREAT IN SHIMLA AND THE RASHTRAPATI NILAYAM IN HYDERABAD THAT HE VISITS EVERY YEAR. ALL THESE RESIDENCES WERE BUILT BY THE BRITISH FOR THE VICEROY.

THE RASHTRAPATI BHAVAN, PARLIAMENT HOUSE AND NORTH & SOUTH BLOCK, ALL LOCATED ON RAJPATH IN NEW DELHI, WERE DESIGNED BY TWO BRITISH ARCHITECTS EDWIN LUTYENS AND HERBERT BAKER AS PART OF THE BRITISH EMPIRE'S CAPITAL OF NEW DELHI. THE BRITISH BUILT A NEW CAPITAL CITY AS THEY DECLARED THEY WOULD HAVE A THOUSAND YEAR EMPIRE BUT THEY OCCUPIED THEIR NEW CITY FOR JUST SEVENTEEN YEARS!

B.R. Ambedkar said of the role of the President, 'He is the head of the state but not of the executive. He represents the nation but does not rule the nation.' This means that the President is not involved in the daily running of the government as that is the job of an elected prime minister. It is the prime minister who heads the cabinet and his ministers lead the various government ministries. When a bill is passed by both houses of Parliament it goes to the President for his approval. The bill becomes law only after the President has signed it. The President can send a bill back for Parliament to reconsider it but if it is passed again then he has to sign it. There are two presidential powers that have led to much controversy over the years; one is the power to dismiss a state government and impose President's Rule and the other is the power to impose a state of Emergency.

SENDING IT BACK

EVERY BILL PASSED BY PARLIAMENT HAS TO GO TO THE PRESIDENT FOR HIS APPROVAL AND HE HAS THE RIGHT TO SEND THE BILL BACK FOR A SECOND LOOK. IN 1987, DURING THE GOVERNMENT OF RAJIV GANDHI, PRESIDENT ZAIL SINGH RETURNED A BILL TO THE PARLIAMENT. HE WAS THE FIRST PRESIDENT TO DO SO. THIS WAS WHEN THE CONGRESS PARTY HAD A HUGE MAJORITY IN BOTH THE LOK SABHA AND THE RAJYA SABHA. THE PRESIDENT SENDING BACK A BILL IS TAKEN VERY SERIOUSLY BY THE PARLIAMENT. THERE IS ONE EXCEPTION TO THIS PRESIDENTIAL POWER, IN THE CASE OF MONEY BILLS LIKE THE ANNUAL BUDGET, THE PRESIDENT CANNOT SEND BACK A BILL.

The real executive power is vested in the council of ministers, headed by the prime minister. The leader of the party that wins a majority of seats in the Lok Sabha is invited by the President to form the government and he becomes the prime minister. The prime minister then chooses his team—the Council of Ministers, including Cabinet Ministers and Ministers of State. A minister who is not a member of Parliament has to win an election or get nominated to the Rajya Sabha within six months. Some of the important ministries are of Home, Finance, Defence, Health, Telecommunications and Human Resource Development. The last is the ministry that handles education and that affects the lives of all Indian children.

Elections are held every five years for the legislative assemblies of the states, and the leader of the largest party becomes the chief minister, who then forms his government. The executive in the states is headed by the Governor and he is not elected but appointed by the President.

PRESIDENTIAL RULE

A GOVERNOR OF A STATE CAN RECOMMEND A PRESIDENTIAL RULE IF THE GOVERNMENT IS NOT FUNCTIONING PROPERLY. THEN THE GOVERNOR HEADS THE GOVERNMENT TILL NEW ELECTIONS ARE HELD WITHIN SIX MONTHS. THE CONSTITUTION MAKES IT CLEAR THAT THERE CAN BE PRESIDENTIAL RULE IN THE STATES BUT IT DOES NOT ALLOW THAT IN THE CENTRE. THIS IS AIMED AT PROTECTING THE COUNTRY FROM A PRESIDENT TAKING OVER ALL POWER AND BECOMING A DICTATOR.

VOICES

'THE BEDROCK OF THE NATIONALIST MOVEMENT WAS THE CLAIM THAT INDIANS WERE NOT INFANTS; THEY WERE CAPABLE OF SELF-GOVERNMENT.'
—PRATAP BHANU MEHTA

Jawaharlal Nehru understood the power of the post of the prime minister and described it as the 'linchpin of the government'. The prime minister is the active head of the executive and exercises real power within the government, and is the link between the cabinet ministers, the legislature and the President. The role of the prime minister is a bit like the principal of your school, who supervises every function of the school and keeps an eye on the performance of the teachers. The prime minister can be a member of either the Rajya Sabha or the Lok Sabha. Manmohan Singh, who never stood for elections, was a member of the Rajya Sabha during his two terms as prime minister.

PRIME MINISTERS

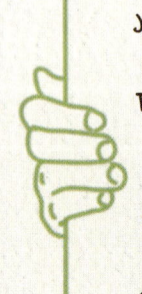

THE FIRST PRIME MINISTER OF INDIA, JAWAHARLAL NEHRU, HOLDS THE RECORD OF THE LONGEST SERVING PRIME MINISTER; HE SERVED FOR SEVENTEEN YEARS. THE FIRST AND, SO FAR, THE ONLY WOMAN PRIME MINISTER WAS HIS DAUGHTER INDIRA GANDHI. GULZARILAL NANDA BECAME ACTING PRIME MINISTER TWICE—ONCE AT THE DEATH OF JAWAHARLAL NEHRU IN 1964 AND THE SECOND TIME AT THE SUDDEN DEATH OF LAL BAHADUR SHASTRI IN 1966.

The prime minister is the leader of the political party that has the majority in the Lok Sabha. This can also be a coalition of many parties. It is the prime minister who decides on the portfolio of the ministers and is free to change them any time he wants, through a process popularly called a reshuffle of portfolios. He presides over all meetings of the cabinet and keeps track of the work of all the ministries and regularly meets the President to give him reports of the work of the government.

So the executive arm of the government is the President, the prime minister and the council of ministers. In the same way, in the states, it is the Governor of the State, the chief minister and his cabinet. Every government has ministries and departments handling different areas from education and health to defence and the finances. At the village level of administration, we have the panchayats, which are an old tradition.

Mahatma Gandhi was very keen to have the government run at the village level but the Constituent Assembly felt that panchayats were not democratic. In the old system, the panchayats were dominated by the rich landowners and the poor farmers; Dalits and women had no say and were often exploited by the rich. However, by the rules of the Panchayati Raj, elections are held to select the members of the panchayat. They serve for five years and there are seats reserved for women. At the district level, we have the Zilla Parishad that oversees the work of the panchayats.

The Legislature: The Lok Sabha, Rajya Sabha, Legislative Assembly

The legislature means the Parliament. In India, we have two houses of Parliament—the Lok Sabha, often referred to as the Lower House and the Rajya Sabha, referred to as the Upper House; though in fact, it is the Lower House that truly represents the people and has more power. The Rajya Sabha means the 'Council of the States' and the Lok Sabha is the 'House of the People'. Our Parliament functions from the Parliament House or Sansad Bhavan in New Delhi.

TWO HOUSES

SOME COUNTRIES HAVE TWO HOUSES OF PARLIAMENT CALLED BICAMERAL AND SOME HAVE ONE CALLED UNICAMERAL. IN GREAT BRITAIN, THE TWO HOUSES OF PARLIAMENT ARE THE HOUSE OF COMMONS AND THE HOUSE OF LORDS. IN THE UNITED STATES OF AMERICA, IT IS THE HOUSE OF REPRESENTATIVES AND THE SENATE. SWITZERLAND HAS ONE HOUSE CALLED THE FEDERAL DIET; AND ISRAEL HAS THE KNESSET. CHINA'S SINGLE HOUSE CALLED THE NATIONAL PEOPLE'S CONGRESS HAS A LONG CHINESE NAME—QUANGUO RENMIN DAIBIAO DEHUI!

Exactly what does the Parliament do? The Prime Minister and his council of ministers come from the two houses of Parliament, and it is the job of the members to monitor their work. The opposition is made up of members of political parties that are not in power and it is their job to keep a close watch on the functioning of the government. Members often ask questions that the minister has to reply. The Parliament makes new laws and amends or even repeals old laws. One of its most important functions is to manage the finances of the country, which is handled by the finance ministry.

SOUNDS LIKE PARLIAMENT IS IN SESSION!

At the Budget Session, the Finance Minister presents the budget for the next year and both houses discuss and ask questions about it. All the sessions are supervised by the Speaker who controls the proceedings; deciding who will speak and for how long. Considering how our members of Parliament often behave, shouting and invading the well of the house, the job of the Speaker is a hard one. Usually, when the members of the Lok Sabha or the Rajya Sabha vote for or against a bill, the Speaker does not vote. However, if there is a tie, the Speaker is allowed to vote. So far, this has never happened.

MADAM MINISTER

WOMEN HAVE HELD MANY MINISTERIAL POSTS IN THE CABINET. OF THE IMPORTANT CABINET POSTS THERE HAVE BEEN TWO WOMEN FINANCE MINISTERS AND DEFENCE MINISTERS SO FAR—INDIRA GANDHI AND NIRMALA SITHARAMAN.

The election for the Rajya Sabha is different from that of the Lok Sabha, the people do not vote in a general election. The Rajya Sabha has 250 members, of whom 238 are elected by the members of the Vidhan Sabhas, the State legislative assemblies. Twelve members are nominated by the President and these are usually eminent citizens. This is how famous people, such as the writer Khushwant Singh, singer Lata Mangeshkar and actress Shabana Azmi became Rajya Sabha members. Each member gets a term of six years but every two years, one-third of the Upper House retires. The Vice President is the Chairperson of the Upper House and conducts the proceedings.

THREE SESSIONS

THREE SESSIONS ARE USUALLY HELD OF THE PARLIAMENT: BUDGET SESSION (FEBRUARY-MAY); MONSOON SESSION (JULY-AUGUST) AND WINTER SESSION (NOVEMBER-DECEMBER). ALL THE SESSIONS ARE BROADCAST LIVE ON LOK SABHA AND RAJYA SABHA TELEVISION.

The members of the Lok Sabha are elected directly by the people for a term of five years. This is the general elections, when Indians wait patiently in queues to vote and come out with a smear of ink on their left forefinger and a big happy smile. The winning candidate is the one who gets the maximum votes even though this may be less than half the votes cast. This happens because multiple candidates divide up the vote. This has often led to a political party winning the elections even though less than fifty percent of the voters voted for them. The Lok Sabha has 552 members, and of these, two seats are nominated from the Anglo-Indian community. The Speaker officiates over the proceedings of the Lower House and usually, he or she is elected from the majority party. Within the Lok Sabha and Rajya Sabha, the Speaker's word is final.

ALL WOMEN

IN 2009, INDIA HAD A NUMBER OF WOMEN
HEADING POSTS IN THE PARLIAMENT AND
EXECUTIVE. PRESIDENT PRATIBHA PATIL WAS
THE FIRST WOMAN PRESIDENT OF INDIA AND
MEIRA KUMAR BECAME THE FIRST WOMAN
SPEAKER OF THE LOK SABHA. SONIA GANDHI,
AS THE PRESIDENT OF THE CONGRESS
PARTY, WAS THE LEADER OF THE PARTY
IN PARLIAMENT.

All bills have to be passed by both Houses and it is then sent for the assent of the President and bills can be introduced in any house. A bill, which is like a proposal, can be introduced by any member in either house of Parliament. Once it is passed and signed by the President, it becomes an act of Parliament. During an Emergency, the Lok Sabha's term can be extended by one year at a time but new elections have to be held within six months of the ending of the Emergency. This has happened only once, in 1976.

The Judiciary: The Supreme Court, High Court

The Constitution created three arms of the government—the executive, the legislature and the judiciary. The architects of the Constitution made sure that they have equal power and that they act as a counter balance against any excesses by one section. They were very conscious of how tempting absolute power could be. For example, a political party having a majority in both houses of Parliament could try to change the Constitution. Or in a time of war, a President could be tempted to declare an Emergency, dismiss the government and hold on to all the power. History has shown that even leaders who began as freedom fighters and democrats could become dictators. So this system of checks and balances between the executive, legislature and the judiciary was crucial.

The judiciary is the protector of the rights of the citizens. It interprets the laws, passes judgement in legal disputes and plays a very important role in defending the Constitution from being challenged by the executive or the legislature. It is the job of the judiciary to make sure that the government functions within the Constitution. That is why the founders of our Constitution made sure that our judiciary was independent of the control of even the prime minister and the President.

The judicial system is like a pyramid, with the Supreme Court at the top. Below are High Courts in the States and then subordinate courts. The Supreme Court is headed by the chief justice who is appointed by the President. And usually, he is the senior-most judge in the court. During the Emergency, this convention was ignored by Indira Gandhi, who wanted an obedient chief justice; four of the senior judges were not appointed to the top post, causing them all to resign in protest. There was great criticism by the people at what was seen as an attack on the independence of the judiciary as well as the Constitution. So far, no other government has dared to do it again.

How is a judge selected for the Supreme Court? Right now, it is through a system called the collegium. A group led by the chief justice and with the four senior-most judges of the Supreme Court select new judges. Their names are then sent to the law ministry and if, for any reason, the ministry does not approve, then the name goes back to the collegium. However, if the collegium approves the name for the second time, the law ministry cannot stop the appointment—a similar system is followed in the states for the appointment of High Court judges. However, a judge retires at the age of sixty-five, unlike the Supreme Court of the United States where the judges are appointed for life.

YOUR HONOUR!

THE FIRST CHIEF JUSTICE OF INDIA WAS JUSTICE HARILAL JEKISUNDAS KANIA WHO TOOK OFFICE IN 1950. THERE HAVE BEEN WOMEN JUDGES IN THE SUPREME COURT BUT THEY HAVE NOT SERVED AS CHIEF JUSTICE. THE FIRST WOMAN JUDGE TO BE APPOINTED TO THE SUPREME COURT WAS FATHIMA BEEVI IN 1989. TILL DATE, THERE HAVE BEEN EIGHT WOMEN JUDGES AND THE LATEST APPOINTMENTS HAVE BEEN INDU MALHOTRA AND INDIRA BANERJEE.

The Constitution gives Indian citizens the right to appeal directly to the Supreme Court if their fundamental rights have been threatened in any manner. They do not have to struggle through the lower courts for this. The Supreme Court also decides all matters of conflict between the

Centre and the States and intervenes in conflicts between States. One of the examples is the matter of the division of the waters of the River Kaveri between Karnataka and Tamil Nadu.

One of the most powerful rights given to the common man is the Public Interest Litigation (PIL). Any citizen can appeal to the Supreme Court if they feel their Fundamental Rights have been threatened, for example, a powerful political leader threatening someone. We can appeal to the Supreme Court even when a matter does not affect us directly but are concerned about an injustice taking place. A Public Interest Litigation (PIL) can be sent by an ordinary post card and the honourable court will take it into consideration.

A JUDGE RETIRES

ONCE A SUPREME COURT JUDGE RETIRES, THEY CAN NO LONGER PLEAD BEFORE ANY COURT AS LAWYERS. THIS HAS BEEN DONE TO ENSURE THE INDEPENDENCE OF THE JUDICIARY.

The problem with our judiciary is the time it takes for a case to be decided. At times, it can take decades, as the courts are burdened with a huge backlog of cases. There are not enough courts and many posts of judges are often not filled on time. At the same time, quite a few of our laws are outdated and need to be changed. Hence, the Indian judicial system needs urgent reforms.

The Babu Log

The prime minister appoints a finance minister who presents a budget in Parliament and it is passed by the two houses. It will have new taxes and budgets for all the ministries and plans for national projects. Now how will all these plans and proposals be put to work? That is the work of the members of the civil service and the government officials in various ministries and departments. For a country of the size of India and its huge population, running it is a very complex operation. For example, take the Indian Railways which is among the largest in the world with thousands of railway stations, a network of railway lines on which chug along thousands of trains carrying crores of passengers. One minister of railways, sitting in Delhi, could not do the job alone, could he?

AN INDIAN MARVEL

THE NUMBERS ARE AMAZING! THE INDIAN RAILWAYS IS THE FOURTH-LARGEST RAILWAY NETWORK IN THE WORLD. IT HAS A NETWORK OF TRACKS OF ROUTE LENGTH OF 67,368 KILOMETRES AND A TOTAL TRACK LENGTH OF 1,21,407 KILOMETRES. AS OF 2018, THERE ARE 7,349 RAILWAY STATIONS SPREAD ACROSS INDIA FROM KASHMIR IN THE NORTH TO KANYAKUMARI IN THE SOUTH, FROM AHMEDABAD IN THE WEST TO GUWAHATI IN THE EAST.

Many of us would be surprised to know that during the rule of the British, the actual exercise of colonial power was mostly in the hands of Indians. The Indian Civil Service (ICS) was originally an all-British cadre and they headed the administration of the country. These were the district magistrates and revenue officers who came in contact with people and they were the human face of the colonial government, the 'mai baap' of the villagers. However, below them, the superstructure from clerks and peons to officers in the various departments was staffed by Indians. Gradually, Indians were allowed to join the elite service and by 1947, even the ICS had many Indian officers.

As historian Bipan Chandra points out, during the freedom movement, our leaders often criticized the ICS for being, 'a small elite group of overpaid, insensitive, mostly British men'. So it was presumed that once we gained independence, our government would dismantle the whole structure. But no one had anticipated the utter chaos that followed independence, with the partition of the country. There was a gigantic movement of the population and horrific violence, and at the same time, there was a war in Kashmir as Pakistan invaded the State. Then there was the assassination of Mahatma Gandhi. At that time, the one organization that was essential was a stable and functioning administrative service and another problem was that most of the British bureaucrats had left for Britain.

The Home Minister Sardar Patel recommended that the ICS be retained and the Constituent Assembly supported his practical plan. It was now renamed the Indian Administrative Service (IAS), and its role is spelled out in Part XIV of the Indian Constitution, headed by the words, 'Service under the Union and the States'. New officers were needed urgently and so, an independent commission to appoint new officers was set up to ensure that the selection was fair and impartial. This is the Union Public Service Commission; it holds annual examinations and selection of the services, like the Indian Administrative Service and the Police Service.

Studying the history of the Constitution of India in action is like watching a film of the evolution of the life of Indians. One big achievement is that even the poorest Indian has a sense of democracy and has the understanding of equality and fundamental rights. However, we are still a society that is divided and unequal and we have still not

MANY SERVICES

ORIGINALLY, ONLY THE INDIAN ADMINISTRATIVE SERVICE (IAS) AND THE INDIAN POLICE SERVICE (IPS) WERE ESTABLISHED. IT WAS FOLLOWED BY THE INDIAN FOREST SERVICE AND THE INDIAN ENGINEERING SERVICE.

learnt the simple value of religious tolerance. As historian Bipan Chandra says wisely, 'We cannot lay our failures at the door of the Constitution; where there are failures, as indeed there are many, it is not the Constitution that has failed us, it is we who have failed the Constitution.'

As President Rajendra Prasad said at the time of the framing of the Constitution, 'A Constitution can only be as good as the people who work it.'

CHAPTER SEVEN

INDIA BECOMES A REPUBLIC

'[Universal adult suffrage is] the gong, the
single note, whose reverberation might
awaken—or at least stir—sleeping India.'

GRANVILLE AUSTIN

The greatest symbol of a democracy is what is called universal adult suffrage. That sounds a bit complicated but what it really means is one citizen, one vote. It is the greatest gift of our Constitution to the people of India. We take it for granted but it was not that common in the world in 1947. There were many countries that did not give the vote to women and Switzerland only voted for women's suffrage in 1971! African Americans in the United States did not have the vote in many southern states. And in 1950 a large part of Asia and Africa was still colonized, where people had no vote anyway.

India was the first colony to gain independence and all the other colonies were watching our drafting of the Constitution and our first elections very carefully. Meanwhile, the west, especially the colonizers, had grave misgivings about Indians being able to understand elections. What they forgot was that we had fought a long drawn out struggle to gain independence, during which the people of India had learnt the value of democratic systems, equality and liberty. The men and women marching out to face the police were often poor and illiterate but they knew the meaning of freedom.

No political system places as much power in people as universal adult franchise. Communism, the other political system that was tried in the twentieth century, began with great ideals but it had one flaw, it did not allow the growth of many political parties like we have in India. This led to the dictatorship of one party and empowered very few. Democracy is not perfect; at times, it can be rather messy and confusing but is the best system we have.

LET US VOTE

THE UNITED STATES OF AMERICA BECAME A DEMOCRACY IN 1789 WHEN ITS CONSTITUTION CAME INTO FORCE. IT FOUGHT A CIVIL WAR TO FREE THE SLAVES BUT TILL THE TWENTIETH CENTURY, MANY OF THE DESCENDANTS OF THE SLAVES WERE DENIED THE RIGHT TO VOTE. IN THE SOUTHERN STATES, LIKE ALABAMA AND MISSISSIPPI, THE STATE LEGISLATURES THAT SUPPORTED SEGREGATION PASSED LAWS REFUSING THE VOTE TO AFRICAN AMERICANS.

IN THE 1960S, THERE WAS A HUGE SURGE OF PROTESTS BY AFRICAN AMERICANS LED BY REV. MARTIN LUTHER KING. YOUNG PEOPLE ENTERED RESTAURANTS WHERE, EVEN WHEN THEY WERE NOT SERVED, THEY REFUSED TO LEAVE; OTHERS WENT AND SAT ON THE FRONT SEATS OF BUSES THAT WERE RESERVED FOR WHITES. THIS PEACEFUL PROTEST WAS INSPIRED BY MAHATMA GANDHI'S SATYAGRAHA. THE PROTESTERS FACED VIOLENCE, BOMBINGS, EVEN ATTACKS BY THE POLICE. MANY DIED BUT THEY DID NOT GIVE UP. AFTER THE FAMOUS MARCH FROM SELMA TO MONTGOMERY IN 1965, THE GOVERNMENT PASSED THE VOTING RIGHTS ACT, ENSURING AFRICAN AMERICANS HAD THE RIGHT TO VOTE.

Since the Constitution was first adopted, we have surprised the world and shown how even an illiterate, landless labourer and his wife understand their right to vote and at least once every five years, exercise this right with the maturity of a resident of a free and democratic country. Of course, we have to admit that even seventy years later, the process is not perfect. Voters often face the threats of powerful political leaders, bribes are offered to them and they are asked to vote according to their caste or religion and many of them agree. Still, when they are alone in the cubicle with the voting machine, they often vote thoughtfully. For example, in 1977, to the shock of the Congress party, Indira Gandhi was defeated because of her imposition of the Emergency, when people's fundamental rights had been taken away. Often in the past elections, voters have surprised political pundits with their votes and our politicians have learnt not to take the voter for granted.

The Congress Party had wanted universal adult suffrage from as early as the 1920s, showing its faith in the common man. There were many suggestions for indirect elections, like the one that Mahatma Gandhi was keen on—through panchayats. However, an overwhelming majority of the Constituent Assembly voted for adult suffrage. As a matter of fact, it was the only Article that was passed without any vote of dissent. So today, every Indian over the age of eighteen, man or woman, rich or poor, educated or not, of every religion and every region gets one vote.

The Indian voter has learnt that through their vote, they can make the powerful listen. They can let the political leaders know if they are angry or happy at the performance of the government. That is why, at least once every five years, even the most powerful leader will come to them begging for their vote and if their promises have not been kept, even the humblest citizen, standing at the door of his village hut in a dhoti and kurta, can make them listen. That is why our finest leaders, like Jawaharlal Nehru, Lal Bahadur Shastri and Atal Bihari Vajpayee, never forgot the people who voted them to power and what they owe the Indian citizen.

VOICES

'TO GIVE EVERYBODY A RIGHT TO VOTE IS A REMARKABLY BOLD MOVE IN RETROSPECT, BECAUSE IF YOU LOOK AT THE HISTORY OF VOTING PRIVILEGES IN WESTERN SOCIETIES, IT DIDN'T HAPPEN IN ONE DAY. HERE, WE TRIED A BIG BANG APPROACH.'
—NANDAN NILEKANI

The general election is the best example of our Constitution in action and that is why the country gets so excited about it. Most amazingly, in an unequal, caste-dominated and patriarchal society, the power of the vote has started a social revolution. The Dalits and tribal people have now understood that in India, no one is a subject of another and people have slowly learnt about the value of equality. These social changes are slow and it is easy to feel disheartened when we see poverty is still far from being eradicated or when a Dalit or a Muslim is killed because of his/her caste or religion. It is our duty as fellow citizens to protest loudly when we see such injustice and we have to continue our fight for them. Fortunately, the Constitution, and the Supreme Court as its guardian, stand with us, the citizens.

WE DID HAVE ELECTIONS

DURING THE RULE OF THE BRITISH, AFTER THE GOVERNMENT OF INDIA ACT OF 1935 ELECTIONS WERE HELD FOR THE GOVERNMENT OF THE PROVINCES IN 1936 BUT NOT EVERYONE HAD VOTING RIGHTS. THERE WERE MANY RESTRICTIONS ACCORDING TO INCOME AND EDUCATION AND NO WOMAN HAD THE RIGHT TO VOTE; SO ONLY ABOUT 15 PER CENT OF THE ADULT POPULATION COULD VOTE. OF COURSE, IN THE PRINCELY STATES, THE IDEA OF ELECTIONS DID NOT EXIST. OUR MAHARAJAS AND NAWABS WOULD HAVE BEEN SHOCKED AT SUCH A REVOLUTIONARY IDEA!

The First Elections in 1952

When the first elections were held between October 1951 and March 1952, every Indian experienced democracy first hand. Elections for the Lok Sabha and all the State Assemblies were held together, to make the job even more challenging. Like it is today, it was the biggest voting exercise in the world with 17.3 crore voters, and since a majority of them lived in villages, they had but the faintest idea what democracy or elections meant. So unlike today, most people back then were first time voters and they had to be taught how to vote.

The election involved lakhs of voters in a country the size of a subcontinent with a daunting landscape of mountains, forests, deserts and islands. Just the working team of the Election Commission was of ten lakh election workers who had to compile the first voter's list by going from house to house; village to village, and to town and city localities. Then there was the setting up of voters' booths; manufacturing ballot boxes; printing ballot papers; training election officers; voting and the counting of votes, and all this at a time when the government had very little money. Also, don't forget that this was a time when there were no computers, Internet or email. There were just post and telegraphs, very few telephones and typewriters, so everything had to be done carefully by hand. It was a mammoth task that was quite scary in its scale. It was at this first election that it was proved that when we Indians want to do a job well, we can do it.

COWS ASK FOR VOTES

THE ELECTION SYMBOL OF THE CONGRESS WAS A COW AND A CALF. DURING THE ELECTION CAMPAIGN, PEOPLE IN CALCUTTA NOTICED THAT MANY STRAY COWS WANDERING AROUND IN THE STREETS HAD THEIR BACKS PAINTED WITH THE WORDS, 'VOTE CONGRESS' IN BANGLA. ONE VOTING BOOTH IN A REMOTE ORISSA REGION WAS NOT VISITED BY ANY VOTER BUT TWO LEOPARDS AND AN ELEPHANT WANDERED PAST, CHECKING OUT THE ACTION.

SUBHADRA SEN GUPTA

This election was Jawaharlal Nehru's show as, with typical energy and passion, he criss-crossed the country addressing up to three huge rallies every day. What was even more remarkable was that at these rallies, he was speaking less about voting for the Congress and more about democracy. From one village hamlet to another, he was busy educating people about their rights. How they were not just free but also equal and they should vote without fear. In all, he covered nearly forty-thousand kilometres and addressed 3.5 crore people; travelling by road, train, air and by boat. Nehru enjoyed meeting people and the whole campaign rejuvenated him. It was as if he was single handedly lighting the lamp of democracy in the country. There was no hate in his speeches, no criticism of other political parties, no attempt to divide people; just the joy of saying, we are free, let's vote and build our own government.

JUST NUMBERS!

- The 1952 elections were for 489 Lok Sabha seats and 3283 State Assembly seats.
- There were 14 national parties and 63 regional parties.
- The total number of voters was over 17.3 crore.
- Over 70 per cent of the voters were illiterate.
- We needed 25 lakh steel ballot boxes and nearly 62,00,00,000 ballot papers.
- They were used at 2,24,000 polling booths.
- 8.1 crores or 46.6 per cent votes were cast.

- The Congress won 364 out of 489 seats; that is 75 per cent of the seats in the Lok Sabha.
- 16,500 clerks typed out the electoral rolls and used up 3,80,000 reams of paper.
- All the votes were counted by hand.

Sukumar Sen (1898–1963)

Working away behind the scenes was another remarkable man—Sukumar Sen, the first election commissioner who had the challenging task of organizing such a huge exercise. In the elections that took place between 1951 and 1952, to the Lok Sabha and the State legislatures, Nehru was seriously worried about the cost. For example, lakhs of steel ballot boxes had to be manufactured, ballot papers had to be printed and then transported all across India. Then, as most people could not read, symbols had to be designed for the political parties.

Sen was a mathematician who had won a gold medal from the University of London and joined the ICS. He was appointed India's first chief election commissioner and faced a very daunting task. First of all, a voter's list of over 17.3 crore people, living all across India, had to be compiled from scratch! Nehru was in a hurry to hold the elections but Sen refused to speed up the process and Nehru bowed to his better judgement. In those days, the bureaucracy was given the freedom to do their job without interference and so Nehru let him set the schedule.

Sen was a tough bureaucrat, going strictly by the rules. For example, during the house to house survey, many women in north India, with its patriarchal society, refused to give their own names, just saying they were some man's mother, sister or wife. Sen did not allow these women to vote and he was criticized for that but he was right. But during the next elections, these very same women forgot their shyness, proudly gave their names and then voted for the first time in their lives, often with their faces covered of course! Sen was chief election commissioner from 1950 to 1958, and administered the first two elections successfully. Historian Ramachandra Guha calls him, 'an unsung hero of Indian democracy'. He was awarded the Padma Bhushan for his great work.

The elections were spread over four months and everywhere, people turned voting day into a festival as they arrived at polling booths, often packed into bullock carts, dressed in their finest clothes. Simple villagers confounded all experts by voting thoughtfully and carefully, and there was quite a low percentage of invalid votes. The Congress Party won an overwhelming majority with 75 per cent of the seats in the Lok Sabha and 68.5 per cent in the State Assemblies. Jawaharlal Nehru then took oath of office as the first Prime Minister of the Republic of India.

The Elections Now

When India held its fifteenth general elections for the Lok Sabha in 2009, it was also getting ready to celebrate sixty years as a republic the following year. The country had confounded a sceptical world by remaining a democracy. The programme of voting is the largest and most complex exercise in the world. Today, every citizen over the age of eighteen years is eligible to vote and in 2009, which meant over 71 crore voters. Unnao in Uttar Pradesh, with 18 lakh voters, was the largest constituency and Lakshadweep was the smallest with just 44,000. People voted for a total of 8070 candidates and the fact that there were only 556 women candidates compared to 7514 men shows how our society stills remains deeply patriarchal and unequal.

At the sixteenth election in 2014, there were over 81.4 crore eligible voters. Uttar Pradesh, with eighty seats, had 13.4 crore voters and Sikkim, had 30 lakhs. Malkajgiri in Andhra Pradesh, with 29 lakh voters, was the largest constituency and Lakshadweep, with 47,000, the smallest. In the seventeenth elections of 2019, there were about 90 crore voters, so in the next elections, we could hit the 100-crore mark!

The Election Commission decided that no voter should have to walk more than two kilometres to reach a polling booth. In 2009, out of the 8,00,000 polling stations, there was one set up in Banej, deep in Gujarat's Gir forest for a single voter—Bharatdas Darshandas, who is the priest at the Ban Gangeshwar Mahadev temple. In another polling station in the Sonhat forest of Chhattisgarh, polling officers waited for two voters. At every election, polling officers walk through forests, cross rivers by boat and trek in the hills to reach voters, and that includes the teams that go to the highest polling station in India at Auley Phu in Ladakh. These nameless people are the real heroes of our democracy.

UNLIKE US, PEOPLE
ELECT THEIR LEADERS!
SO STRANGE!!

VOTE FOR ME

IN 2009, AMONG THE CANDIDATES WHO FILED THEIR PAPERS WERE A MOGAMED ALI JINNAH, ARUN KENNEDI, HARAPPA MOHENJODARO AND D. NAPOLEON. AT TIMES POLITICAL PARTIES PUT UP CANDIDATE WITH IDENTICAL NAMES TO THAT OF AN OPPOSITION CANDIDATE TO CONFUSE THE VOTER.

How have the elections evolved from 1952? The election in 2019 was for 545 seats and the voter turnout was of 67.47 per cent. There were many new elements from the time of Nehru. First was the social media, which made election campaigns both wider and also full of worrying matters like false news. Now, of the 2856 candidates, 464 had criminal cases filed against them. There were 90 crore eligible voters and that was 8.4 crores more than in 2014, making this the largest election in the world. In India's first general elections, the minimum age for a voter was twenty-one years but it is now eighteen years and there were 1.5 crore first-time voters. Voters were also allowed to identify as the third gender.

In the 1951–1952 elections, as most voters were illiterate, ballots were put in tin boxes with the party symbol on them. At the next elections, the symbols were printed on the ballot papers. Now we have the electronic voting machines (EVM) that were first used in 1997. In

2014, the voter verified paper audit trail (VVPAT) was introduced, which shows the vote on paper. We also have a vote called 'none of the above' or NOTA. Of course, somethings remain unchanged, like the indelible ink smeared on the left forefinger.

Symbols of the Republic

As we all raise our voices singing the National Anthem and proudly watch the tricolour go up the flag pole, we are saluting symbols of the Republic of India, which were chosen by the Constituent Assembly. The Assembly approved a national flag, an anthem, a song and a visual icon of our new republic. So the tricolour became our national flag, the anthem was 'Jana Gana Mana'; the song 'Vande Mataram' and the icon was of the three Ashokan lions.

The Indian flag has three bands of colour—saffron on top, white in the middle and green at the bottom. In the centre, on the white band, is the twenty-four-spoke Ashoka Chakra in dark blue. The flag is always made of hand-spun khadi cloth. President S. Radhakrishnan explained the significance of the three colours. Saffron stands for sacrifice and the spirit of renunciation; white is the light to the path of truth and the green is our connection to plants and our soil. The Ashoka Chakra is the law of Dhamma.

Over the years, there were many efforts to design a flag of India. The flag we know now was designed by Pingali Venkayya (1876–1963), a freedom fighter and educationist from Andhra Pradesh. He designed it for the Congress and it had a charkha in the centre that was replaced by the

Ashoka Chakra in 1947. He did see his design become the flag of the new nation but the Congress forgot all about him and Venkayya died in poverty.

FIRST STAMP

BEFORE EMAILS EXISTED, WE WROTE LETTERS ON PAPER, USING A PEN AND INK. WE WOULD SEAL THEM INSIDE AN ENVELOPE, FIX A STAMP ON IT AND POST IT IN A LETTER BOX. THE FIRST STAMP OF INDEPENDENT INDIA SHOWS OUR FLAG, THE DATE 15 AUGUST 1947, THE WORDS 'JAI HIND' AND WAS PRICED AT THREE AND A HALF ANNAS. THE SECOND STAMP SHOWED THE ASHOKA LIONS.

Our National Anthem 'Jana Gana Mana' was written by poet and Nobel Laureate Rabindranath Tagore. He first sang the song at the Calcutta (Kolkata) session of the Indian National Congress in 1911. The National Song 'Vande Mataram' was written by the novelist Bankim Chandra Chatterjee in his novel 'Anandamath' that was published in 1882. The Lion Capital of Ashoka, which we see on all official Government of India papers and on our currency notes, was discovered at Sarnath. It has the words 'Satyameva Jayate', truth alone triumphs, written below the lions. So two of our symbols—the Ashoka Chakra on the flag and the Lion Capital are connected to the great Mauryan king Ashoka.

POET EXTRAORDINAIRE

RABINDRANATH TAGORE IS THE ONLY POET IN THE WORLD WHOSE SONGS HAVE BECOME THE NATIONAL ANTHEMS OF TWO COUNTRIES. WE SING 'JANA GANA MANA' AND IT IS A JOYOUS SONG OF PRAISE OF OUR BEAUTIFUL LAND. IN BANGLADESH, THEY SING THE LOVELY, 'AMAR SHONAR BANGLA' WHICH IS A PAEAN TO THE LAND OF BENGAL. THE ANTHEM OF SRI LANKA, COMPOSED BY ANANDA SAMARAKOON, IS SAID TO HAVE BEEN INSPIRED BY THE POETRY OF TAGORE.

The First Republic Day Parade

On our first Republic day—26 January 1950, President Rajendra Prasad came out of Rashtrapati Bhavan and got into the silver and black horse-drawn buggy that at one time carried the British Viceroy. As the President's bodyguards, sitting ramrod straight on their horses, clip-clopped down Raisina Hill, the significance of the moment was not lost on the delighted spectators.

This was the President of the Indian people, not the viceroy who was the representative of a colonial power. He was the head of the state of an independent nation who was driving down the broad avenue we named Rajpath, which was once called Kingsway. Then the tricolour went up to the beat of the National Anthem as cannons boomed out a twenty-one-gun salute. Since then, on every chilly 26th January morning, we watch a parade that Pandit Nehru, the balladeer of our freedom movement called a 'moving pageant' of the country.

The parade starts at Rajpath and ends at the Red Fort. Soldiers march past, bands play, school children in bright costumes dance and a series of tableaux from the states roll by, all creating a vibrant, many hued portrait of our nation. Before the parade, as bugles play below the arch of the India gate, the prime minister lays flowers at the Amar Jawan Jyoti, the eternal flame dedicated to the memory of the Unknown Soldier. The dramatic finale of the parade is the fighter planes of the Indian Air Force streaking across the sky in a breathtaking fly-past. The celebrations come to a close with the melodious notes of the 'Beating Retreat' as the bands of the armed forces sway and march down the slope of the Raisina Hill, as the sun dips behind the dome of the Rashtrapati Bhavan. Here, the last tune that is always played is what is said to be Mahatma Gandhi's favourite hymn, 'Abide With Me'.

WELCOME NELSON MANDELA

INDIA HAD ALWAYS SUPPORTED THE FREEDOM STRUGGLE IN SOUTH AFRICA AND THE AFRICAN NATIONAL CONGRESS' BATTLE AGAINST APARTHEID. AFTER SOUTH AFRICA GAINED INDEPENDENCE, PRESIDENT NELSON MANDELA WAS THE CHIEF GUEST AT THE REPUBLIC DAY CELEBRATIONS IN 1995.

When we chose democracy in 1950, we began a huge adventure that would transform our political life and our society and there have been many ups and downs. We have progressed and sometimes failed at the challenges that we face as a nation. We should end with the practical words of the man who looked at the past, present and future without any illusions. B.R. Ambedkar knew India well and said, 'By independence, we have lost the excuse of blaming the British for anything going wrong. If hereafter things go wrong, we will have nobody to blame except ourselves.'

So as Ambedkar reminds us, this is our nation, this is our Constitution—a gift from the freedom fighters who took back our nation from the long years of colonial rule—and it is for us keep the flame of democracy alive.

STRUCTURE OF THE CONSTITUTION

The Constitution is not just about Fundamental Rights or the form of government. Other topics include citizenship, official language, panchayats, property, contracts and suits. Also subjects like trade, commerce and tribunals were covered. Elections, Amendments and Emergency provisions were covered in twenty-two parts and 395 Articles. A lot of it is very complex and hard to understand. It looks like the Constituent Assembly tried to think of every aspect of a citizen's life and also anticipate what the future will bring.

OFFICIAL LANGUAGE OF INDIA

This topic was a source of loud, angry and excited debates in the Assembly. Some linguists say that India has nearly a thousand languages and local dialects. So which language could be made the official language? After much debate, Hindi was chosen since it was the most commonly spoken language, but that decision led to protests in many parts of India, especially in South India. So English was also allowed for official communications.

The Constitution then allowed the states to adopt any of the other languages for official purposes. Really, for practical reasons, English is the language that is understood by the maximum of people. So in the Parliament, the government or the Supreme Court, it continues to be used.

The twenty-two official languages listed in the 8th Schedule are Assamese, Bengali, Bodo, Dogri, Gujarati, Hindi, Kannada, Kashmiri, Konkani, Maithili, Malayalam, Manipuri, Marathi, Nepali, Odia, Punjabi, Sanskrit, Santhali, Sindhi, Tamil, Telugu and Urdu.

ELECTION SYMBOLS

With so many political parties, the Election Commission really struggles to design symbols. Among the strange symbols are a lock and key for the All India United Democratic front; a bungalow for the Lok Jan Shakti Party and a pair of spectacles for the Indian National Lok Dal. Even food items have been included like a banana for the AJSU Party and two coconuts of the Karnataka Janatha Paksha. The Aam Aadmi Party has a broom; Pattali Makkal Katchi Party a mango and the Rashtriya Lok Dal a handpump. Sometimes, there is confusion between the Bahujan Samaj party and the Asom Gana Parishad since they both have the elephant as a symbol. So if a BSP candidate stands from Assam, they will have to choose another symbol.

FOOD FLAG

Sometimes, we get confused about the bands of colours in the Indian flag. Is the saffron on top or is it the green? Here's a foody way to remember. Imagine a meal being served in Tamil Nadu or Karnataka, on a banana leaf. On top is the golden-yellow sambar; in the middle is the snowy white rice and below is the green coriander and mint chutney. Then to complete the picture, place a crisp round murukku in the middle of the band of rice. Deeelicious!

MORE FASCINATING FACTS

- The Constituent Assembly took two years, eleven months and seventeen days to draft the Constitution.
- So far, no woman has been elected as the vice-president of India.
- The President stays in the Rashtrapati Bhavan. The official residence of the State Governor is called Raj Bhavan. Rashtrapati Bhavan was the Viceroy House and the Kolkata Raj Bhavan was the residence of the governor-general.
- The Prime Minister's Office (PMO) is located in the South Block of the two Secretariat buildings that flank the Raisina Hill that goes up to Rashtrapati Bhavan.
- The official vehicles of the President and the Governors only have the national emblem on the number plate.
- After Independence, states were created on the basis of language as this would make the work of administration easier. In 1959, the first such state was Andhra Pradesh (Telugu) followed by Kerala

(Malayalam); Karnataka (Kannada); Maharashtra (Marathi) and Gujarat (Gujarati).

- Three new States were created in 2000—Chhattisgarh carved out of Madhya Pradesh, Uttarakhand from Uttar Pradesh and Jharkhand from Bihar.

- Among the important Articles is Article 17, which abolishes untouchability. Article 330 provides for reservations of seats for schedules castes and scheduled tribes in the Lok Sabha.

- A television series called 'Samvidhan' was produced by Lok Sabha Television, directed by Shyam Benegal and has Swara Bhaskar as the narrator of the story of the creation of the Indian Constitution. Look for it on YouTube.

- At the International Socialist Congress at Stuttgart in 1907, the freedom fighter Bhikaiji Cama unfurled a flag that had a green band on top with a row of eight white lotuses; a yellow band in the middle with the words 'Bande Mataram' in Hindi; and an orange band in the bottom with a half moon and a sun.

- To discover more about the Constitution of India just go to Google.

- Wikipedia has many sections on the Constitution of India that are worth going through.

- Also check the website of Rashtrapati Bhavan. It has some lovely photographs of the building, the Mughal Gardens and the President's Bodyguards.

MORE READING!
MORE FUN!

If this book has got you interested in the story of our freedom movement and on the writing of the Constitution I do recommend you dip into the following books. They are full of amazing facts and the stories of extraordinary people. Also if you have questions or criticism you can always email me: subhadrasg@gmail.com. I promise to reply.

1. *The Indian Constitution: Cornerstone of a Nation* by Granville Austin. Oxford University Press
2. *India After Independence* by Bipan Chandra et al. Penguin
3. *India After Gandhi: The History of the World's Largest Democracy* by Ramachandra Guha. Picador
4. *We, the Children of India* by Leila Seth. Puffin.
5. *Derek Introduces the Constitution and Parliament of India* by Derek Obrien. Rupa
6. *A Children's History of India* by Subhadra Sen Gupta. Rupa.

7. *Saffron, White and Green: The Amazing Story of India's Independence* by Subhadra Sen Gupta. Puffin

8. *A Flag, a Song and a Pinch of Salt: Freedom Fighters of India* by Subhadra Sen Gupta. Puffin.

9. *Puffin Lives: Mahatma Gandhi, the Father of the Nation* by Subhadra Sen Gupta. Puffin

10. *Jawaharlal Nehru* by Aditi De. Puffin